Collins

AQA GCSE 9-1
Maths
Foundation

T0337578

Leisa Bovey

Acknowledgements

The authors and publisher are grateful to the copyright holders for permission to use quoted materials and images.

Every effort has been made to trace copyright holders and obtain their permission for the use of copyright material. The authors and publisher will gladly receive information enabling them to rectify any error or omission in subsequent editions. All facts are correct at time of going to press.

All images ©Shutterstock and HarperCollins*Publishers*

Published by Collins
An imprint of HarperCollins*Publishers* Limited
1 London Bridge Street
London SE1 9GF

HarperCollins*Publishers*
Macken House
39/40 Mayor Street Upper
Dublin 1
D01 C9W8
Ireland

© HarperCollins*Publishers* Limited 2024

ISBN 978-0-00-867237-9

First published 2024

10 9 8 7 6 5 4 3 2 1

British Library Cataloguing in Publication Data.

A CIP record of this book is available from the British Library.

Author: Leisa Bovey
Publisher: Clare Souza
Commissioning and Project Management: Richard Toms
Editorial: Richard Toms, Anne Stothers and
Laura Connell (Maven Publishing)
Inside Concept Design: Ian Wrigley
Layout: Jouve India Private Limited and Nicola Lancashire
(Rose & Thorn Creative Services Limited)
Cover Design: Sarah Duxbury
Production: Bethany Brohm

Printed in India by Multivista Global Pvt.Ltd.

MIX
Paper | Supporting
responsible forestry
FSC
www.fsc.org
FSC™ C007454

This book contains FSC™ certified paper and other controlled sources to ensure responsible forest management.

For more information visit: www.harpercollins.co.uk/green

How to use this book

Organise your knowledge with concise explanations and examples

Key points highlight fundamental ideas

Each topic is presented on a two-page spread

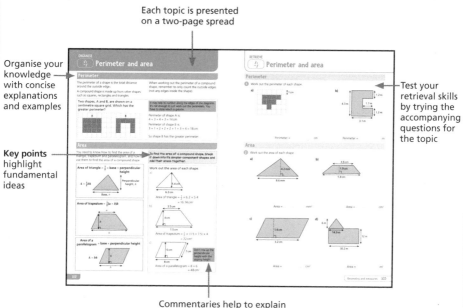

Test your retrieval skills by trying the accompanying questions for the topic

Commentaries help to explain the mathematical steps

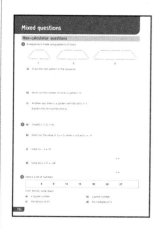

Mixed questions further test retrieval skills after all topics have been covered

Key facts and vocabulary section helps to consolidate knowledge of mathematical terms and concepts

Answers are provided to all questions at the back of the book

Contents

Contents

④ Geometry and measures

⑤ Probability

⑥ Statistics

Positive and negative numbers

Positive and negative numbers

Positive numbers are greater than zero and **negative numbers** are less than zero. They can be shown on a number line.

An **integer** is a whole number. It can be positive, negative or zero. −5, 0 and 3 are examples of integers.

Adding and subtracting with negative numbers

Remember:
- adding a positive number increases the answer
- subtracting a positive number decreases the answer
- adding a negative number decreases the answer; it is the same as subtracting a positive number.
- subtracting a negative number increases the answer; it is the same as adding a positive number.

> Subtracting a negative number is the same as adding a positive number.

The average temperature in Prague in December is 3°C. The average temperature in Moscow in December is 6°C less than in Prague. Work out the average temperature in Moscow in December.

$3 - 6 = -3$

Average temperature in Moscow in December is −3°C.

a) Work out 3 − 5.

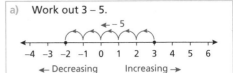

Starting at 3 and decreasing by 5 gives:
$3 - 5 = -2$

b) Work out 2 − (−4).

Starting at 2 and increasing by 4 gives:
$2 - (-4) = 2 + 4 = 6$ ← ⊖ ⊖ = ⊕

c) Work out 5 + (−6).

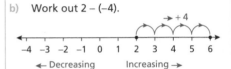

Starting at 5 and decreasing by 6 gives:
$5 + (-6) = 5 - 6 = -1$ ← ⊕ ⊖ = ⊖

Multiplying and dividing with negative numbers

When multiplying and dividing with negative numbers:
- if the signs are the same, the answer is positive
- if the signs are different, the answer is negative.

Work out:

a) 7×-8

$7 \times -8 = -56$ ← + × − = −

b) -9×-2

$-9 \times -2 = 18$ ← − × − = +

c) $-30 \div 6$

$-30 \div 6 = -5$ ← − ÷ + = −

d) $-25 \div -5$

$-25 \div -5 = 5$ ← − ÷ − = +

Positive and negative numbers

Positive and negative numbers

1. Draw arrows to show where the following numbers lie on the number line.

   a) 5

   b) −3

   c) 2

   d) −7

Adding and subtracting with negative numbers

2. Work out:

   a) −3 − 4

   b) 7 − (−2)

   c) −8 + 6

   d) −1 + (−1)

Multiplying and dividing with negative numbers

3. Work out:

   a) −4 × −3

   b) 9 × −2

   c) −12 ÷ 2

   d) −21 ÷ −7

(1) Written calculations

Addition and subtraction

To add and subtract **integers**, line up the digits by place value and add or subtract each of them, starting with the ones.

When adding, you may need to carry to the next column on the left. When subtracting, you may need to exchange from the next column on the left.

Work out 356 + 72.

```
    3  5  6
 +     7  2
   ─────────
    4  2  8
    1
```

Start from the right-hand side.
6 + 2 = 8. Write **8** down.

5 + 7 = 12. Write **2** down and carry **1**

3 + 1 = 4. Write **4** down.

Work out 438 – 57.

```
    ³4 ¹3  8
 −      5  7
   ─────────
    3  8  1
```

Start from the right-hand side.
8 − 7 = 1. Write **1** down.

3 is less than **5**. Exchange 100 from the hundreds column for tens to give **13 − 5 = 8**. Write **8** down.

3 − 0 = 3. Write **3** down.

Multiplication

Column multiplication:
1. Write the number with the highest place value on top and line up the digits by place value.
2. Working from right to left, multiply the ones of the bottom number by each digit of the top number. If the product is more than 10, carry the tens digit.
3. Repeat for the tens of the bottom number. Do the same for all the digits of the bottom number.
4. Add up the results of each multiplication.

For column multiplication, don't forget to include a zero in each row of the addition to show multiplication by tens, hundreds, etc. This is sometimes called a place holder.

Work out 364 × 14.
Column multiplication

```
        3  6  4
 ×         1  4
   ───────────────
    1  4₂ 5₁ 6
    3  6  4  0
   ───────────────
    5₁ 0  9  6
```

Work out 364 × 4
Work out 364 × 10
Add the two multiplications together.

Grid method:
1. Partition the numbers into their place values. Write one partitioned number on top of the grid and the other to the side.
2. Multiply each part.
3. Add up the numbers inside the grid.

Grid method

×	300	60	4	
10	3000	600	40	3640
4	1200	240	16	+ 1456
				5096

Division

Write the number being divided (the **dividend**) inside the box and the number you are dividing by (the **divisor**) outside the box. The answer (the **quotient**) goes on top of the box. Divide each place value of the dividend by the divisor, starting with the largest place value.

Short division:
1. Divide each place value of the dividend by the divisor, starting with the largest place value.
2. If the divisor does not go into the dividend, write a zero above that place value. Write the remainder next to the next digit, carrying over.
3. Keep dividing until you have divided every place value of the dividend.

```
        0  1  3  8
 1  2  1 ¹6 ⁴5 ⁹6
```

Long division:

Long division is similar to short division. It just involves showing your working to find the remainder at each place value rather than carrying it over at each step.

1. Divide
2. Multiply
3. Subtract
4. Bring down

```
           0  1  3  8
  1  2 |  1  6  5  6
       −  1  2  ↓
       ─────────
            4  5
          − 3  6  ↓
          ───────
               9  6
```

① Written calculations

Addition and subtraction

1 Work out the following without a calculator.

a)
```
  3 1 2
+ 4 6 9
```

b) 1782 + 53

c)
```
  9 3 6
- 8 5 4
```

d) 1284 − 38

Multiplication

2 Work out the following using your preferred written method.

a)
```
  3 8 5
×   4 2
```

b) 89 × 14

c)
```
  2 5 3
×   3 7
```

d) 47 × 39

Division

3 Work out the following. Use either long or short division.

a) 7 ⟌ 5 7 4

b) 3396 ÷ 12

c) 16 ⟌ 8 4 8

d) 3969 ÷ 18

1 Fractions (1)

Simplifying and equivalent fractions

A **fraction** represents part of a whole.

$\dfrac{3}{4}$ ← numerator
← denominator

Equivalent fractions can be simplified to the same value. A fraction is **simplified** when the numerator and denominator have no common factors (other than 1).

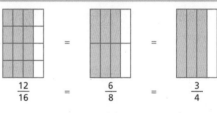

$$\frac{12}{16} = \frac{6}{8} = \frac{3}{4}$$

Mixed numbers and improper fractions

A **mixed number** is a fraction and an integer.

An **improper fraction** has a denominator greater than the numerator.

  $1\frac{2}{3} = \frac{5}{3}$

To convert an improper fraction to a mixed number:

1. Divide the numerator by the denominator and leave the remainder.
2. The whole number is the integer part of the mixed number.
3. The remainder is the numerator of the fraction. The denominator stays the same.

To convert a mixed number to an improper fraction:

1. Multiply the denominator by the whole number.
2. Add the numerator – this becomes the numerator of the improper fraction. The denominator stays the same.

Convert $\frac{7}{3}$ to a mixed number.

$7 \div 3 = 2$ remainder 1, so $\frac{7}{3} = 2\frac{1}{3}$

Convert $3\frac{5}{8}$ to an improper fraction.

$3\frac{5}{8} = \frac{(8 \times 3) + 5}{8} = \frac{29}{8}$

Adding and subtracting fractions

To add or subtract fractions, the denominator must be the same.

1. Rewrite the problem using equivalent fractions with a common denominator.
2. Add or subtract the numerators. Keep the denominator the same.
3. Simplify if possible.

Work out $4\frac{1}{4} - 2\frac{1}{2}$

$4\frac{1}{4} - 2\frac{1}{2} = 4\frac{1}{4} - 2\frac{2}{4}$

$= \frac{17}{4} - \frac{10}{4}$

$= \frac{7}{4} = 1\frac{3}{4}$

$4\frac{1}{4} = \frac{(4 \times 4) + 1}{4} = \frac{17}{4}$ and

$2\frac{2}{4} = \frac{(4 \times 2) + 2}{4} = \frac{10}{4}$

When adding and subtracting mixed numbers, you can either **partition** or **convert to improper fractions**.

Work out $2\frac{2}{3} + 1\frac{1}{2}$

Partitioning

$2\frac{2}{3} + 1\frac{1}{2} = 2 + 1 + \frac{2}{3} + \frac{1}{2}$

$= 3 + \frac{4}{6} + \frac{3}{6}$ ← $\frac{2}{3} = \frac{4}{6}$ and $\frac{1}{2} = \frac{3}{6}$

$= 3 + 1\frac{1}{6}$ ← $\frac{4}{6} + \frac{3}{6} = \frac{7}{6} = 1\frac{1}{6}$

$= 4\frac{1}{6}$

Converting to improper fractions

$2\frac{2}{3} + 1\frac{1}{2} = \frac{8}{3} + \frac{3}{2}$

$= \frac{16}{6} + \frac{9}{6}$

$= \frac{25}{6}$

$= 4\frac{1}{6}$

$2\frac{2}{3} = \frac{(3 \times 2) + 2}{3} = \frac{8}{3}$ and

$1\frac{1}{2} = \frac{(2 \times 1) + 1}{2} = \frac{3}{2}$

1 Fractions (1)

Simplifying and equivalent fractions

1 Fill in the missing values for these equivalent fractions.

$$\frac{16}{20} = \frac{}{10} = \frac{40}{} = \frac{}{5}$$

2 Simplify:

a) $\frac{8}{20}$ ....

b) $\frac{9}{21}$ ....

c) $\frac{21}{28}$ ....

d) $3\frac{4}{18}$ ....

Mixed numbers and improper fractions

3 Convert the mixed numbers to improper fractions.

a) $3\frac{1}{4}$ ....

b) $2\frac{5}{8}$ ....

4 Convert the improper fractions to mixed numbers.

a) $\frac{18}{5}$ ....

b) $\frac{21}{8}$ ....

Adding and subtracting fractions

5 Work out and simplify where possible:

a) $\frac{3}{5} + \frac{2}{10}$ ....

b) $\frac{2}{3} + \frac{5}{8}$ ....

c) $3\frac{1}{3} + 4\frac{3}{4}$ ....

d) $2\frac{3}{8} + 1\frac{1}{2}$ ....

6 Work out and simplify where possible:

a) $\frac{5}{7} - \frac{3}{14}$ ....

b) $\frac{4}{5} - \frac{1}{8}$ ....

c) $3\frac{1}{2} - 2\frac{1}{3}$ ....

d) $5\frac{2}{3} - 3\frac{1}{8}$ ....

7 Tina makes $2\frac{3}{8}$ litres of squash. She and her friends drink $1\frac{3}{4}$ litres.

How much squash is left?

1 Fractions (2)

Multiplying fractions

1. Change any mixed numbers to improper fractions.
2. Multiply the numerators together.
3. Multiply the denominators together.
4. Simplify the answer if possible.

a) Work out $\frac{3}{4} \times \frac{3}{5}$ $\frac{3}{4} \times \frac{3}{5} = \frac{9}{20}$

b) Work out $2\frac{2}{3} \times 1\frac{1}{5}$ $2\frac{2}{3} \times 1\frac{1}{5} = \frac{8}{3} \times \frac{6}{5}$

Simplify by cancelling by 3 $= \frac{8}{3^1} \times \frac{6^2}{5}$

$= \frac{16}{5} = 3\frac{1}{5}$

Dividing fractions

1. Convert any mixed numbers to improper fractions.
2. Remember **KFC**:
   Keep the first fraction as it is
   Flip the second fraction
   Change ÷ to ×

Remember to flip the second fraction when dividing fractions.

a) Work out $\frac{5}{6} \div \frac{3}{5}$ $\frac{5}{6} \div \frac{3}{5} = \frac{5}{6} \times \frac{5}{3}$

$= \frac{25}{18} = 1\frac{7}{18}$

b) Work out $1\frac{1}{4} \div 2\frac{1}{3}$ $1\frac{1}{4} \div 2\frac{1}{3} = \frac{5}{4} \div \frac{7}{3}$

$= \frac{5}{4} \times \frac{3}{7} = \frac{15}{28}$

Fractions of amounts

Working out a fraction of an amount:
1. Divide by the denominator.
2. Multiply by the numerator.

Work out $\frac{2}{5}$ of 25.
$\frac{2}{5}$ of $25 = (25 \div 5) \times 2$
$= 5 \times 2$
$= 10$

$\frac{3}{4}$ of the 28 students in a class are boys. How many are girls?

You can either work out $\frac{1}{4}$ of 28 for the number of girls or $\frac{3}{4}$ of 28 for the number of boys and then subtract this from the total number of students.

$\frac{3}{4}$ of $28 = \frac{3}{4} \times 28$
$= \frac{3}{4^1} \times \frac{28^7}{1} = 21$

There are 21 boys, so $28 - 21 = 7$ girls

Writing one quantity as a fraction of another:
1. Write the amounts using the same units.
2. Write the fraction. The numerator is the amount, and the denominator is the 'out of' number.

Write 30 cm as a fraction of 1 metre.

1 metre = 100 cm ← Make the units the same.

So 30 cm as a fraction of 1 metre is

$\frac{30 \text{cm}}{100 \text{cm}} = \frac{3}{10}$

In two tests, Nicholas gets 13 out of 15 and 16 out of 20. Which is the better score?

To compare the two scores, write them as fractions with common denominators. Then compare the numerators.

13 out of 15 is $\frac{13}{15} = \frac{52}{60}$ ← Multiply the numerator and denominator by 4

16 out of 20 is $\frac{16}{20} = \frac{48}{60}$ ← Multiply the numerator and denominator by 3

So 13 out of 15 is the better score.

1 Fractions (2)

Multiplying fractions

1 Work out:

a) $\frac{2}{3} \times \frac{5}{8}$

b) $2\frac{1}{3} \times 3\frac{3}{4}$

c) $1\frac{3}{8} \times 2\frac{1}{4}$

Dividing fractions

2 Work out:

a) $\frac{3}{4} \div \frac{1}{3}$

b) $\frac{4}{7} \div \frac{3}{5}$

c) $2\frac{2}{5} \div 1\frac{1}{8}$

d) $3\frac{3}{4} \div \frac{2}{3}$

Fractions of amounts

3 a) Work out $\frac{1}{3}$ of 30

b) Work out $\frac{3}{8}$ of 24

4 a) Write 15 cm as a fraction of 1 m.

b) Write 30 mg as a fraction of 15 g.

5 $\frac{3}{5}$ of a class of 30 students buy school dinners. The rest take a packed lunch.

How many students take a packed lunch?

1 Decimals

Place value

This place value table shows the number 1234.567

The digit 5 has a value of 5 tenths or $\frac{5}{10}$

Thousands	Hundreds	Tens	Ones	.	tenths	hundredths	thousandths
1	2	3	4	.	5	6	7

Write these numbers in ascending order:	2.33, 23.03, 3.022, 32.02, 2.303
2.330, 23.030, 3.022, 32.020, 2.303	Rewrite the numbers to the same number of decimal places.
2.303, 2.33, 3.022, 23.03, 32.02	Compare and order from lowest to highest by place value. Then write each number to the original number of decimal places.

Adding, subtracting, multiplying and dividing decimals

To add and subtract decimals:
1. Rewrite the numbers so that they have the same number of decimal places.
2. Line up the decimal points.
3. Add or subtract as usual.

Work out: a) 5.83 + 2.6   b) 3.4 − 1.28

	5	.	8	3
+	2	.	6	0
	8	.	4	3
			1	

	3	.	³4	¹0
−	1	.	2	8
	2	.	1	2

To multiply decimals:
1. Multiply the numbers as if the decimal point were not there.
2. Count how many decimal places are in the two numbers.
3. Put the decimal point into the product so that the number of decimal places is the same as the total in the two numbers being multiplied.

Work out 2.34 × 5.1

		2	.	3	4
×		5	.	1	
		2	3	4	
1	1,	7,	0	0	
1	1	.	9	3	4

Three decimal places in the question.

Three decimal places in the answer.

To divide a decimal by an integer:
1. Bring up the decimal point into the answer.
2. Divide.

To divide by a decimal:
1. Count the number of decimal places in the divisor (the 'divided by' number).
2. Multiply both numbers by the power of 10 that will remove the decimal point.
3. Divide.

Work out: Short division is used in these examples.

a)   13.2 ÷ 6

Line up the decimal points.

		2	.	2
6	1	3	.¹	2

So 13.2 ÷ 6 = 2.2

b)   18.312 ÷ 0.6

One decimal place in 0.6 so multiply both numbers by 10.
18.312 ÷ 0.6 is the same as 183.12 ÷ 6

		3	0	.	5	2
6	1	8	3	.³	1	¹2

So 18.312 ÷ 0.6 = 30.52

Changing between decimals and fractions

To change a decimal to a fraction:
1. Look at the smallest place value in the number and write it as the denominator.
2. The numerator is the number without the decimal point. Simplify if possible.

To change a fraction to a decimal:
Divide the numerator by the denominator.

If you see the same digit (or sequence of digits) repeating in the answer, it is a recurring decimal.

Change 0.24 to a fraction in its simplest form.

$0.24 = \frac{24}{100} = \frac{6}{25}$ The smallest place value is hundredths, so use 100 as the denominator.

Change to decimals: Add a decimal point to the divisor and bring it up to the answer.

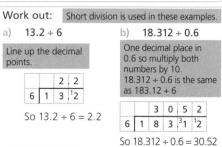

a) $\frac{3}{8}$

	0	.	3	7	5
8	3	.	0	⁶0	⁴0

$\frac{3}{8} = 0.375$

b) $\frac{2}{3}$

	0	.	6	6	6...
3	2	.	0	²0	²0

$\frac{2}{3} = 0.666...$

① Decimals

Place value

1 Order these numbers from least to greatest:

0.805   8.05   0.85   0.588   8.5

Adding, subtracting, multiplying and dividing decimals

2 Work out:

a) $17.99 + 2.3$ **b)** $54.9 - 1.62$

3 Work out:

a) 7.6×6.2 **b)** 10.33×3.7

4 Work out:

a) $42.6 \div 6$ **b)** $67.2 \div 0.7$

Changing between decimals and fractions

5 Change:

a) 0.512 to a fraction

b) $\frac{5}{8}$ to a decimal.

1 Multiples and factors

Multiples and lowest common multiple

Multiples are the numbers in the times table of a given number.

The multiples of 3 are:

$3 \times 1 = 3$

$3 \times 2 = 6$

$3 \times 3 = 9$

$3 \times 4 = 12$

$3 \times 5 = 15$

… and so on.

The multiples of 7 are:

$7 \times 1 = 7$

$7 \times 2 = 14$

$7 \times 3 = 21$

$7 \times 4 = 28$

$7 \times 5 = 35$

… and so on.

Numbers can have many common multiples, but only one lowest common multiple.

Common multiples are multiples that are the same for two given numbers. The **lowest common multiple** (**LCM**) is the smallest of the common multiples. Sometimes the lowest common multiple is one of the numbers itself.

Multiples of 3: 3 6 9 ⑫ 15 18 21 ㉔ …

Multiples of 4: 4 8 ⑫ 16 20 ㉔ 30 36 …

12 and 24 are in both lists. They are two of the common multiples of 3 and 4. The LCM of 3 and 4 is 12.

Multiples of 5: 5 ⑩ 15 ⑳ 25 …

Multiples of 10: ⑩ ⑳ 30 40 50 …

The LCM of 5 and 10 is 10.

Anna and Bella are baking cupcakes. Anna bakes cupcakes in batches of 12 and Bella in batches of 8. How many batches must they each bake before they have made the same number of cupcakes?

Multiples of 8:   8 16 ㉔ 32 40 ….

Multiples of 12:   12 ㉔ 36 48 60 …

$24 \div 12 = 2$ and $24 \div 8 = 3$

Anna must bake 2 batches and Bella must bake 3.

When they have both made 24 cupcakes, they will have made the same amount.

Anna bakes 12 cupcakes in a batch, so divide 24 by 12. Bella bakes 8 cupcakes in a batch, so divide 24 by 8.

Factors and highest common factor

Factors are numbers that divide evenly into another number without a remainder. A **factor pair** is two numbers that multiply to give a certain number. To find the factor pairs, think through the numbers that divide evenly. 1 and the number itself will always be in the list. Then think through 2, 3, 4, etc. until you have found all the factor pairs.

Two or more integers can have factors that are the same, called **common factors**. The highest of these is called the **highest common factor** (**HCF**).

Work out the HCF of 12 and 18.

The factor pairs of 12 are 1×12 2×6 3×4

So the factors of 12 are 1, ②, ③, 4, ⑥, 12

The factor pairs of 18 are 1×18 2×9 3×6

So the factors of 18 are 1, ②, ③, ⑥, 9, 18

2, 3 and 6 are all common factors of 12 and 18.

6 is the highest common factor of 12 and 18.

Work out the factors of 20.

Factor pairs of 20 are 1×20 2×10 4×5

$20 \div 1 = 20$

$20 \div 2 = 10$

$20 \div 3 \rightarrow$ Not an integer

$20 \div 4 = 5$ Stop here as the next option is $20 \div 5 = 4$, which is the same.

The factors of 20 are 1, 2, 4, 5, 10, 20.

The HCF is the greatest number that is a factor of two or more given numbers.

Sophie has a purple ribbon that is 36 cm long and a green one that is 45 cm long. She wants to cut them into equal lengths with no ribbon leftover. What is the longest possible length of each piece?

The factors of 36 are 1, 2, 3, 4, 6, 9, 12, 18, 36.

The factors of 45 are 1, 3, 5, 9, 15, 45.

The HCF of 36 and 45 is 9.

So the longest possible length is 9 cm.

(1) Multiples and factors

Multiples and lowest common multiple

1 Work out the lowest common multiple of:

a) 4 and 6

b) 2 and 5

c) 12 and 30

d) 5 and 15

Factors and highest common factor

2 Work out the highest common factor of:

a) 8 and 12

b) 16 and 72

c) 12 and 15

d) 8 and 20

1 Prime factorisation

Prime numbers

A **prime number** has only the factors 1 and itself.
A **composite number** is a number that is not prime.

Try to memorise the prime numbers up to 100:
2, 3, 5, 7, 11, 13, 17, 19, 23, 29, 31, 37, 41, 43, 47, 53, 59,
61, 67, 71, 73, 79, 83, 89, 97

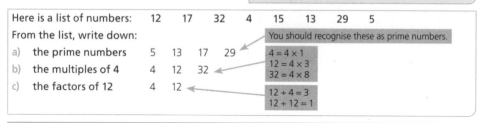

Here is a list of numbers: 12   17   32   4   15   13   29   5

From the list, write down:

You should recognise these as prime numbers.

a)   the prime numbers   5   13   17   29

$4 = 4 \times 1$
$12 = 4 \times 3$
$32 = 4 \times 8$

b)   the multiples of 4   4   12   32

c)   the factors of 12   4   12

$12 \div 4 = 3$
$12 \div 12 = 1$

Prime factorisation

Factors of a number that are prime are called
prime factors. Any integer can be written as all its
prime factors multiplied together and this can be
shown using powers (**index form**).

Any integer can be written as a product of
prime factors.

Write 24 as a product of prime factors.

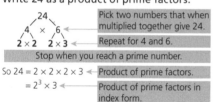

Pick two numbers that when
multiplied together give 24.

Repeat for 4 and 6.

Stop when you reach a prime number.

So $24 = 2 \times 2 \times 2 \times 3$ ← Product of prime factors.

$= 2^3 \times 3$ ← Product of prime factors in index form.

Write 60 as a product of prime factors.

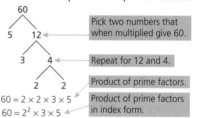

Pick two numbers that
when multiplied give 60.

Repeat for 12 and 4.

Product of prime factors.

$60 = 2 \times 2 \times 3 \times 5$ ← Product of prime factors in index form.

$60 = 2^2 \times 3 \times 5$

Using prime factors to work out the HCF and LCM

To work out the HCF and LCM using prime factors:

1.   Find the prime factors of both numbers.
2.   The HCF is the product of the common prime factors.
3.   The LCM is the product of the HCF and the remaining factors.

Work out the HCF and LCM of 24 and 60.

$24 = ② \times ② \times 2 \times ③$
$60 = ② \times ② \times ③ \times 5$

Draw factor trees for both
numbers. Each product
has two 2s and one 3.

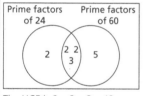

Prime factors of 24   Prime factors of 60

You can use a
Venn diagram
to visualise the
prime factors of
two numbers.

The HCF is $2 \times 2 \times 3 = 12$
The LCM is $12 \times 2 \times 5 = 120$

The lowest common multiple of two
numbers is 24. The highest common factor
of the same two numbers is 4. Work out the
two numbers.

Factors of 24 are   1, 2, 3, 4, 6, 8, 12, 24

Numbers that are also multiples of 4 are
4, 8, 12, 24

Now find pairs where the LCM is 24 and the HCF is 4.

There are two possible answers:
8 and 12   or   4 and 24

Prime factorisation

Prime numbers

1. Here is a list of numbers: 39 16 82 49 83 54 18 61

   From the list, write down the:

   a) prime numbers

   b) multiples of 3

   c) square numbers.

Prime factorisation

2. Write these numbers as products of prime factors.

   a) 32   **b)** 40

   c) 18   **d)** 120

Using prime factors to work out the HCF and LCM

3. Use prime factors to work out the:

   a) HCF of 32 and 40   **b)** LCM of 32 and 40

① Powers and roots

Powers

A power, or index (plural: indices), is a short-hand way of writing a number multiplied by itself. The power indicates how many times the number is multiplied by itself. The number being multiplied is called the **base**.

When a number is raised to the power of 2, it is **squared** and the result is called a **square number**. When a number is raised to a power of 3, it is **cubed** and the result is called a **cube number.**

$$8^5 = 8 \times 8 \times 8 \times 8 \times 8$$

Base   Power (or index)

In words, this is said '8 to the power of 5'.

$5^3 = 5 \times 5 \times 5 = 125$ '5 cubed'

$2^5 = 2 \times 2 \times 2 \times 2 \times 2 = 32$ '2 to the power of 5'

> You should memorise all the squared numbers up to 15^2 and the cube numbers up to 5^3.

Working with powers

The laws of powers:
- To multiply powers of the same number (base), add the powers
  $3^5 \times 3^2 = 3^{5+2} = 3^7$
- To divide powers of the same base, subtract the powers
  $3^5 \div 3^2 = 3^{5-2} = 3^3$
- To raise a power of a number to another power, multiply the powers
  $(3^5)^2 = 3^{5 \times 2} = 3^{10}$
- Any number to the power of 1 is itself
  $3^1 = 3$
- Any number to the power of 0 is 1
  $3^0 = 1$

a)   Write $6^4 \times 6^5$ as a single power of 6.

   $6^4 \times 6^5 = 6^{(4+5)} = 6^9$

b)   Write $5^8 \div 5^4$ as a single power of 5.

   $5^8 \div 5^4 = 5^{(8-4)} = 5^4$

c)   Simplify $\dfrac{4^6 \times 4^2}{4^5}$ $\dfrac{4^6 \times 4^2}{4^5} = \dfrac{4^8}{4^5} = 4^3$

d)   Simplify $\dfrac{3^8 \times 3^3}{3^7}$ $\dfrac{3^8 \times 3^3}{3^7} = \dfrac{3^{11}}{3^7} = 3^4$

> Make sure you know how to find powers and roots on your calculator.

Roots

The **root** of a given number is the number that is multiplied by itself to result in the given number.

The **square root** of a given number is the number that is squared to result in the given number.

The **cube root** of a given number is the number that is cubed to result in the given number.

For example: $\sqrt{9} = 3$ because $3^2 = 9$

   $\sqrt[3]{64} = 4$ because $4^3 = 64$

SHIFT to use other functions

Squared
SHIFT: Cubed

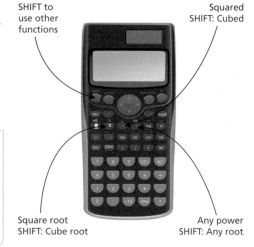

Between which two consecutive numbers does $\sqrt{70}$ lie?

Find the nearest square roots that have a whole number answer. Remember consecutive numbers are next to each other.

$\sqrt{64} = 8$ and $\sqrt{81} = 9$

So $\sqrt{70}$ is between 8 and 9.

Square root
SHIFT: Cube root

Any power
SHIFT: Any root

(1) Powers and roots

Powers

1 Without a calculator, write the value of:

a) 3^2 ....

b) 6^2 ....

c) 10^4 ....

2 Using a calculator, write the value of:

a) 2^6 ....

b) 5^4 ....

c) 18^3 ....

Working with powers

3 Simplify the following.

a) $3^4 \times 3^7$ ....

b) $\frac{4^8}{4^2}$ ....

c) $(5^2)^8$ ....

d) $\frac{(7^2 \times 7^6)}{7^3}$ ....

Roots

4 Write down the value of:

a) $\sqrt{49}$ ....

b) $\sqrt{196}$ ....

c) $\sqrt[3]{125}$ ....

5 Between which two consecutive integers does $\sqrt{87}$ lie? ....

1 Rounding and standard index form

Rounding

To round to a given place value (or number of decimal places):

1. Look at the place value (or decimal place) to the right of the given place value.

2. If the digit is greater than or equal to 5, round the digit up.

3. If the digit is less than 5, leave the digit unchanged.

Round 231.6754:

a) **to the nearest ten**
   230

2 3 1.6754 Look at the digit to the right of the tens.
1 is less than 5 so round down.

A place value table can be a useful tool to help you look at the correct digit.

b) **to 1 decimal place**
   231.7

231. 6 754 Look at the digit to the right of the first decimal place.
7 is greater than 5 so round up.

H	T	O		t	h	th	tth
2	3	1	.	6	7	5	4

c) **to the nearest hundredth.**
   231.68

231.6 7 54 Look at the digit to the right of the hundredths.
The digit is 5 so round up.

Significant figures

To round to a certain number of significant figures (s.f.), count the significant figures from left to right and round to that place value.

The first significant figure is the first non-zero digit from the left. A zero is still significant if it is after the first significant figure.

Write 3150 to 2 significant figures.

3①50 The second significant figure is the 1 in the hundreds place.

3①5̲0 Look at the digit to the right. It is 5 so round up.

3150 is 3200 to 2 s.f.

Approximation

Approximation means to work out an estimate that is close to the actual value. Unless told otherwise, use approximations to 1 s.f.

Estimate the value of $\frac{5020}{4.9 \times 20.8}$

$\frac{5000}{5 \times 20} = 50$ Round each number to 1 s.f.

Estimate the value of $\frac{19.7 \times 30.1}{0.59}$ Round each number to 1 s.f.

$\frac{19.7 \times 30.1}{0.59}$ is approximately $\frac{20 \times 30}{0.6}$

$\frac{20 \times 30}{0.6} = \frac{600}{0.6}$ To remove the decimal from this calculation, multiply the numerator and denominator by 10

$\frac{6000}{6} = 1000$

So $\frac{19.7 \times 30.1}{0.59}$ is approximately 1000

Standard index form

A number in standard form is written as a power of 10. It has one digit to the left of the decimal point.

Numbers between 0 and 1 are written to a negative power of 10.

To calculate with numbers in standard form:

1. Change them to ordinary form.
2. Complete the calculation.
3. Change back to standard form.

A number in standard form is written as $a \times 10^n$ where a is $1 \leqslant a < 10$ and n is an integer.

a) **Write 120 in standard form.**

H	T	O	t	h
		1	2	0
1	2	0		

Write down 1.20 and think about what power of 10 you would multiply by to get 120.

120 in standard form is 1.2×10^2

b) **Write 312 000 in standard form.**

3.12×10^5 Digits move five places.

c) **Write 2.1×10^{-4} in ordinary form.**

0.00021 Digits move four places.

① Rounding and standard index form

Rounding

1 Round:

a) 805.997 to 2 decimal places

b) 45 578.920 27 to the nearest hundredth

c) 1243.304 to the nearest tens.

Significant figures

2 Round:

a) 1273.097 to 1 significant figure

b) 107.896 to 2 significant figures

c) 0.007 8064 to 3 significant figures.

Approximation

3 Use approximations to estimate:

a) the value of $\frac{32.8 \times 18.9}{11.9}$

b) the area of a patio measuring 5.87 m by 2.15 m.

_____ m²

4 Bananas cost 27p each. Ella has £9.

Does she have enough to buy 30 bananas?

Standard index form

5 Write the following in standard form.

a) 13 400

b) 0.003 45

(1) Measures and accuracy

Suitable degrees of accuracy

Measurement questions will often ask to give your answer to a suitable or sensible degree of accuracy.

Think about what a reasonable precision for the measurement is and round to that degree.

> A stack of 40 cards is 2.85 cm high. How thick is each piece of card?
> Give your answer to an appropriate degree of accuracy.
>
> 2.85 cm ÷ 40 = 0.07125 cm
>
> 0.07125 cm is 0.7125 mm ◄── It is unlikely you could measure to this degree of accuracy, so give your answer to the nearest tenth of a millimetre.
>
> An appropriate degree of accuracy is 0.7 mm.

2.85 cm

Limits of accuracy

Any measurement is performed to a given degree of accuracy and the actual measurement will be somewhere between two values, an **upper bound** and **lower bound**.

> The limits of accuracy are always plus and minus half of the degree of accuracy.

If a measurement is 123 cm to the nearest centimetre, the exact length is between the measurements that round to 123 cm.

Degree of accuracy is 1 cm. Half of 1 cm is 0.5 cm.

Upper bound is 123 + 0.5 = 123.5 cm

Lower bound is 123 − 0.5 = 122.5 cm

Rounds up to 123 cm   Rounds down to 123 cm

122.5 cm   123 cm   123.5 cm

A tin contains 400 g of beans, measured to the nearest gram. 38 g (to the nearest gram) of beans are removed.

Work out the largest and smallest possible mass of beans left in the tin.

Largest possible mass of beans in tin: 400.5 g

Largest possible mass removed: 38.5 g

Smallest possible mass of beans in tin: 399.5 g

Smallest possible mass removed: 37.5 g

Most beans left = 400.5 g − 37.5 g = 363 g

> Largest possible mass of beans in tin minus smallest possible amount removed.

Least beans left = 399.5 g − 38.5 g = 361 g

> Smallest possible mass of beans in tin minus largest possible amount removed.

A rectangular field measures 23 m by 18 m, measured to the nearest metre.

Work out the largest and smallest possible area of the field.

Largest possible length: 23.5 m

Smallest possible length: 22.5 m

Largest possible width: 18.5 m

Smallest possible width: 17.5 m

> The greatest possible area is the product of the greatest length and the greatest width. The smallest possible area is the product of the smallest length and width.

Largest possible area: 23.5 × 18.5 = 434.75 m²

Smallest possible area: 22.5 × 17.5 = 393.75 m²

① Measures and accuracy

Suitable degrees of accuracy

1 Work out each calculation. Give your answer to an appropriate degree of accuracy.

a) The area of a piece of wood measuring 3.25 m long and 2.83 m wide.

_____ m²

b) The cost per metre of a 15 m length of fabric costing £35.62

£ _____ per metre

Limits of accuracy

2 A crate holds 98 kg of rocks, measured to the nearest kilogram.

Work out the largest and smallest possible values for the mass of rocks.

Largest possible mass: _____ kg

Smallest possible mass: _____ kg

3 A jug is filled with 1.25 litres of water, measured to the nearest hundredth of a litre.

Work out the largest and smallest possible values for the volume of water in the jug.

Largest possible volume: _____ litres

Smallest possible volume: _____ litres

4 A triangular flag has a base of 10 cm and a perpendicular height of 30 cm, both measured to the nearest centimetre.

What is the largest possible area of the flag?

_____ cm²

② Algebraic expressions

Vocabulary

Vocabulary	Meaning	Examples
Variable	A letter that is used to represent any number	x or n
Coefficient	A number that multiplies a variable	$3x$ or $2y$
Constant	A number that does not have a variable attached to it	4 or 8
Term	One part of an expression, equation, formula or identity	$2x - 3y + 4$ has the three terms $2x$, $-3y$ and $+4$
Expression	A combination of variables with numbers and operations	$2x + 3y$ or $\frac{x}{2} + 1$
Equation	Contains an equals sign and at least one variable	$2x + 5 = 16$ or $x + 3y = 7$
Formula	A rule connecting more than one variable; it also has an equals sign	$A = \pi r^2$ or $s = \frac{d}{t}$
Identity	Contains an identity sign and is true for all values	$x + x \equiv 2x$ or $(x + 5)^2 \equiv x^2 + 10x + 25$
Inequality	This is like an equation except that the two sides are **not** equal	$3x - 2 > x + 4$

Simplifying expressions

Like terms are terms that have the same variable. To **simplify** an expression means to combine or collect like terms, e.g. $2x$ and $3x$, or $3k^2$ and $4k^2$.

Terms can be combined if they have the same variables and the same powers.

Are like terms		Are not like terms	
3 and 12	✓	9 and $9x$	✗
$3x$ and $2x$	✓	$3s$ and $4t$	✗
$3xy$ and $2yx$	✓	x^2 and x	✗
$4m^2$ and $3m^2$	✓		

Remember to include the signs in front of the terms when simplifying, and simplify fully.

a) Simplify $3x + 4x$. $3x$ and $4x$ are like terms so can be combined.
$3x + 4x = 7x$

b) Simplify $3k + 4j - 2k + 3j$.
$3k + 4j - 2k + 3j$ Combine the k terms. $3k - 2k = k$
$= 4j + 3j + k$ Combine the j terms. $4j + 3j = 7j$
$= 7j + k$

c) Simplify $x^2 + 4x - 7x + 3x^2$.
$x^2 + 4x - 7x + 3x^2$ $x^2 + 3x^2 = 4x^2$ and $+ 4x - 7x = -3x$
$= 4x^2 - 3x$

d) Simplify $xy + 3yx - 2xy$.
$xy + 3yx - 2xy$ Note that yx is the same as xy.
$= 2xy$

Writing expressions

To write an expression, start by writing in words what the variables represent. Then replace the words with numbers and letters.

For example:
A bag of apples contains 6 apples.
One bag has 6 apples, or 1×6
Two bags have 12 apples, or 2×6
Three bags have 18 apples, or 3×6
n bags have $n \times 6$ apples
An expression for the number of apples in n bags is $6n$.

A rectangle has a width of w. Its length is 2 cm less than its width.

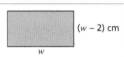

$(w - 2)$ cm

w

Write an expression for the perimeter of the rectangle in centimetres.

The perimeter is found by adding up all the sides, $w + (w - 2) + w + (w - 2) = 4w - 4$

An expression for the perimeter is $4w - 4$ where w is the width of the rectangle.

Remember to state what the variable represents.

② Algebraic expressions

Vocabulary

1 For each of the below, decide whether it is an identity, expression, equation, or inequality.

Then identify the terms, variables, coefficients and any constants for each of them.

	Type	Terms	Variables	Coefficients	Constants
$s^2 + 3su - 4$					
$3k + 4 = 10$					
$2x + 3x \equiv 5x$					

Simplifying expressions

2 Simplify each expression.

a) $3x + 5y - 5x + 3$

b) $4j^2 + 3j - 1 + 2j - 4$

c) $5k - 7 + 3k - 9k + 1$

Writing expressions

3 A regular pentagon has side length x.

Write an expression for the perimeter of the pentagon.

4 A t-shirt costs £15 and trousers cost £25

Write an expression for the cost in pounds of buying s t-shirts and t trousers.

② Substitution

Substituting into expressions

To **substitute** a number into an expression means to replace the given variable with the number.

> Always show your working out when substituting values.

If $x = 2$, $y = -3$ and $z = 0$, work out the value of:

a) $5x - 4y$
$5x - 4y = 5 \times 2 - 4 \times -3$ ◄— Substitute the values for x and y.
$= 10 + 12$ ◄— Show your working out.
$= 22$

b) xyz
$xyz = 2 \times -3 \times 0$ ◄— When variables are written next to each other, it means to multiply them.
$= 0$

c) $y^2 - x$
$y^2 - x = (-3)^2 - 2$ ◄— Use brackets as the minus sign is also squared.
$= 9 - 2$ ◄— Show your working out.
$= 7$

If $x = 3$, $y = -4$ and $z = -6$, work out the value of:

a) $4x + 5y - z$
$= (4 \times 3) + (5 \times -4) - (-6)$ ◄— Substitute the values of x and y. Watch out for the negative sign!
$= 12 - 20 + 6$
$= -2$ ◄— Subtracting a negative value is the same as adding a positive value.

b) xyz
$3 \times -4 \times -6$ ◄— A negative value multiplied by a negative value results in a positive value.
$= 72$

c) $y^2 - \frac{z}{x}$
$= (-4)^2 - \frac{-6}{3}$ ◄— Use brackets around the −4 to show the minus sign is also squared. Follow BIDMAS (see below).
$= 16 + 2$
$= 18$

Substituting into formulae

A **formula** is a rule that relates two or more variables. For example, $A = l \times w$ relates the area of a rectangle to its length and width. To find the area, substitute the length and width.

Remember to follow the order of operations when substituting values.

> **B**rackets
> **I**ndices
> **D**ivision & **M**ultiplication (left to right)
> **A**ddition & **S**ubtraction (left to right)

> To use a formula, substitute the known values in for the variables and calculate.

The formula to work out the cost of a taxi ride is $C = 5 + 1.2m$ where C is the total cost in pounds and m is the number of miles travelled.

Work out the cost of an 8-mile journey.

$C = 5 + 1.2m$
$C = 5 + (1.2 \times 8)$ ◄— Substitute $m = 8$
$C = 5 + 9.6 = 14.6$
The fare is £14.60

The value of money in an account with compound interest can be found using the formula $T = P\left(1 + \frac{r}{100}\right)^n$ where P is the principal (original) amount, r is the interest rate and n is the number of times the interest is added on the account.

Fran puts £1000 into a savings account earning 3% compound interest per year. Calculate the amount in the savings account after 5 years, assuming she does not make any further deposits.

$T = P\left(1 + \frac{r}{100}\right)^n$ ◄— Substitute $P = 1000$, $r = 3$ and $n = 5$

$T = 1000 \times \left(1 + \frac{3}{100}\right)^5$ ◄— Use your calculator.

$T = £1159.274074$ ◄— The question is about money, so round to 2 decimal places.

$T = £1159.27$

② Substitution

Substituting into expressions

1 Substitute the values into each.

a) Work out the value of x if $x = 2y + 4z - 1$ when $y = 4$ and $z = 5$

$x =$ ....

b) Work out the value of R if $R = \frac{3x - 2t}{2}$ when $x = 2$ and $t = 1$

$R =$ ....

Substituting into formulae

2 The formula for speed is $S = \frac{D}{T}$ where S is the speed, D is the distance travelled and T is the time taken.

Work out the speed of a car travelling 240 miles in 4 hours.

.... mph

3 The formula for calculating the volume of a square-based pyramid is $V = \frac{1}{3}(a^2 \times h)$, where V is the volume, a is the side length of the base and h is the perpendicular height.

Shown below is a square-based pyramid that has a base of side length 2 cm and a perpendicular height of 3 cm.

Calculate its volume.

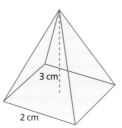

3 cm

2 cm

.... cm^3

② Expanding brackets

One set of brackets

To **expand** (or **multiply out**) **brackets** means to multiply each term within the brackets using the **distributive law**.

You can expand the brackets by using a grid but you can use another method if you prefer.

The distributive law
$$a(b + c) = ab + ac$$
$$a(b - c) = ab - ac$$

Grid method	Without a grid
1. Draw a grid split into the same number of parts as there are terms.	1. Multiply the term outside the brackets by each term inside the brackets.
2. Partition the terms in the bracket and write them on top of the grid.	2. Simplify.
3. Write the term that is outside the bracket on the side of the grid.	It can help to draw arrows or lines from the outer term to the inner terms as you multiply to keep track of your working.
4. Multiply each part and simplify.	

Expand $3(2x - 4)$

Grid method

Partition into $2x$ and 4.

×	2x	−4
3	6x	−12

$= 6x - 12$

$3 \times 2x = 6x$ $3 \times -4 = -12$

Multiply each term.

Without a grid

$3(2x - 4) = (3 \times 2x) + (3 \times -4)$
$$= 6x - 12$$

Multiply the 3 by each term inside the bracket.

Make sure you multiply by each term inside the bracket.

Two sets of brackets

To multiply or expand two sets of brackets, you must multiply everything from the first by everything in the second. You can use a grid to help you. Alternatively, when both brackets have two terms you can use the acronym FOIL to help you keep track of the terms.

Multiply **every** term in the first bracket by **every** term in the second bracket.

Grid method	FOIL method
1. Partition the terms in both brackets.	**F**irsts: multiply the first terms.
2. Write the terms from one bracket on the top of the grid.	**O**uters: multiply the outer terms.
3. Write the terms of the other bracket to the side.	**I**nners: multiply the inner terms.
4. Multiply each part and find the sum.	**L**asts: multiply the last terms.

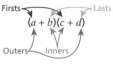

Multiply out $(2x + 3)(x - 1)$

Grid method

Partition each bracket and multiply each term.

×	2x	3
x	2x²	3x
−1	−2x	−3

$= 2x^2 + 3x - 2x - 3$

$= 2x^2 + x - 3$

Using FOIL

$(2x + 3)(x - 1) = (2x \times x) + (2x \times -1) + (3 \times x) + (3 \times -1)$
$$= 2x^2 - 2x + 3x - 3$$
$$= 2x^2 + x - 3$$

(2) Expanding brackets

One set of brackets

1 Expand:

a) $4(j - 5)$

b) $-2(k - 1)$

c) $3(2m + 4)$

2 Expand and simplify $3(x - 3) - 2(x + 4)$

Two sets of brackets

3 Multiply out:

a) $(x - 3)(x + 5)$

b) $(2x + 1)(3x - 5)$

c) $(2m - 3)(3m + 1)$

2 Factorising expressions

Factorising

To **factorise** means to write an expression as a multiplication, or to pull out a common factor.

To factorise using a grid:
1. Write the terms of the expression inside the grid.
2. Find the HCF of the terms. Write it outside the grid.
3. Divide each term by the HCF. Write the result on top of the grid.
4. Write the final answer in brackets.

To factorise without a grid:
1. Find the highest common factor (HCF) of all the terms in the expression.
2. Divide each term by the HCF.
3. Write the HCF outside the brackets and the result of step 2 inside the brackets.

Factorise:

a) $3x + 6$

$3x \div 3 = x \quad 6 \div 3 = 2$

	x	2
3	$3x$	6

$= 3(x + 2)$

HCF of $3x$ and 6

$3x + 6 = 3(x + 2)$

b) $4x^2 + 3x$

	$4x$	3
x	$4x^2$	$3x$

$= x(4x + 3)$

HCF of $4x^2$ and $3x$

$4x^2 + 3x = x(4x + 3)$

c) $8xy - 6x^2$

	$4y$	$-3x$
$2x$	$8xy$	$-6x^2$

$= 2x(4y - 3x)$

HCF of $8xy$ and $-6x^2$

$8xy - 6x^2 = 2x(4y - 3x)$

Quadratic expressions of the form $x^2 + bx + c$

Using a grid:
1. Write the x^2 term in the top left.
2. Write the c term in the bottom right.
3. Find two terms that multiply to cx^2 and add to bx.
4. Write those terms in the empty spots in the grid.
5. Find the HCF of each row and column of the grid.
6. Write the result in brackets.

Without a grid:
1. Write two brackets with x as the first term in both, $(x \quad)(x \quad)$.
2. If c is negative, one number will be positive and the other negative.
3. Find two numbers that multiply to c and add to b.
4. Write those two numbers as the second term in the brackets.

Factorise:

a) $x^2 - x - 12$

With a grid

HCF of x^2 and $-4x$

HCF of $3x$ and -12

HCF of x^2 and $3x$ →

HCF of $-4x$ and -12 →

	x	3
x	x^2	$3x$
-4	$-4x$	-12

$3x \times -4x = -12x^2$

$3x - 4x = -x$

$x^2 - x - 12 = (x + 3)(x - 4)$

b) $x^2 + 5x + 6$

Without a grid

$x^2 + 5x + 6 = (x + \ )(x + \ )$ ← c is positive.

$= (x + 2)(x + 3)$ ← Write +2 and +3 in the brackets.

Difference of two squares

A quadratic expression that is the difference of two squares (in the form $a^2 - b^2$) can be quickly factorised into $(a + b)(a - b)$.

Factorise $x^2 - 9$.

Using the difference of two squares ← Recognise that x^2 is a square number and so is 9.

$x^2 - 9 = (x + 3)(x - 3)$

② Factorising expressions

Factorising

1 Factorise:

   a) $2x + 4$

   b) $3a + 9b$

   c) $5x + 20xy$

Quadratic expressions of the form $x^2 + bx + c$

2 Factorise:

   a) $x^2 + 4x + 3$

   b) $k^2 + k - 6$

   c) $x^2 - 3x - 4$

Difference of two squares

3 Factorise:

   a) $x^2 - 16$

   b) $x^2 - 169$

2) Laws of indices

Index notation

An index (plural: indices), or power, is a way of writing repeated multiplication. The same rules apply for powers of variables as for powers of numbers. See page 20 for more on powers and roots.

Power (or index)

$$x^5 = x \times x \times x \times x \times x \times x$$

Base

In words, this is said 'x to the power of 5'.

a) Simplify $x \times x \times x \times x \times x$
$x \times x \times x \times x \times x = x^4$

b) Simplify $j \times j \times j \times j \times j \times j \times j$
$j \times j \times j \times j \times j \times j \times j = j^7$

c) Write m^5 in expanded form.
$m^5 = m \times m \times m \times m \times m$

Simplifying indices

You can simplify expressions with powers of the same variable using the laws of indices, just as you can when the base is a number.

Memorise the laws of indices. To understand how each law works, try writing out a few calculations in expanded form, e.g. $x^2 \times x^3 = (x \times x) \times (x \times x \times x) = x^5$

The laws of indices

In words	In algebra
To multiply powers of the same base, add the powers	$a^m \times a^n = a^{(m+n)}$
To divide powers of the same base, subtract the powers	$a^m \div a^n = a^{(m-n)}$
To raise a power to another power, multiply the powers	$(a^m)^n = a^{(m \times n)}$
Any base to the power of 1 is itself	$a^1 = a$
Any base to the power of 0 is 1	$a^0 = 1$
A negative power means the reciprocal of the power	$a^{-m} = \frac{1}{a^m}$

a) Simplify $x^5 \times x^2$
$x^5 \times x^2 = x^{5+2} = x^7$

b) Simplify $\frac{k^8}{k^2}$
$\frac{k^8}{k^2} = k^{(8-2)} = k^6$

$b^4 \times b^2 = b^{(4+2)}$

$\frac{b^6}{b^8}$ means $b^6 \div b^8$, which is $b^{(6-8)} = b^{-2}$

c) Simplify $(y^3)^2$
$(y^3)^2 = y^6$

d) Simplify $\frac{(b^4 \times b^2)}{b^8}$
$\frac{(b^4 \times b^2)}{b^8} = \frac{b^6}{b^8}$
$= b^{-2}$
$= \frac{1}{b^2}$

A negative power means the reciprocal of the power.

Working with coefficients

Expressions with indices can also have coefficients. Remember the order of operations when dealing with coefficients. $5x^3$ means x is cubed and then multiplied by 5 (the 5 is **not** cubed), whereas $(5x)^3$ means both x and 5 are cubed.

When calculating with indices, deal with any coefficients first and remember BIDMAS.

a) Simplify $3k^2 \times 4k^3$
$3k^2 \times 4k^3 = 12k^5$
$3 \times 4 = 12$ and $k^2 \times k^3 = k^{(2+3)}$

b) Simplify $(3n^4)^2$
$(3n^4)^2 = 3^2 \times n^{4 \times 2} = 9n^8$

Everything inside the brackets is squared.

c) Simplify $\frac{(2p^5 \times p^2)^3}{4p^2}$

$\frac{(2p^5 \times p^2)^3}{4p^2} = \frac{(2p^7)^3}{4p^2}$
$p^5 \times p^2 = p^{5+2}$

$= \frac{8p^{21}}{4p^2}$
$2^3 = 8$ and $(p^7)^3 = p^{(7 \times 3)}$

$= 2p^{19}$
$8 \div 4 = 2$ and $p^{21} \div p^2 = p^{(21-2)}$

2 Laws of indices

Index notation

1 Write each expression in expanded form.

a) x^5

b) $3k^4$

c) $(5j)^3$

Simplifying indices

2 Simplify each expression.

a) $k^2 \times k^8$

b) $\frac{j^8}{j^3}$

c) $\frac{x^3 \times x}{x^5}$

Working with coefficients

3 Simplify each expression, leaving your answer in index form.

a) $2p^5 \times 3p^{-3}$

b) $\frac{(2m)^3 \times m}{4m^2}$

c) $(3k^4)^2 \div k^{10}$

2) Formulae

Using and writing formulae

Remember, a **formula** is a rule that relates two or more variables.

The **subject** of a formula is what you are using the formula to find. It is on its own on one side of the equals sign.

To use a formula, substitute the known values in for the variables and calculate.

$A = l \times w$ relates the area (A) of a rectangle to its length (l) and width (w).

$$A = l \times w$$

Subject   Variables

To find the area, substitute the length and width.

> To write a formula, start by writing it in words then write variables in place of the words.

A taxi service charges a base rate of £6 and an additional £2 per mile travelled.

a) Write a formula for the taxi fare.

The taxi charges £6 + £2 × miles travelled.

As a formula, $C = 6 + 2m$ where m is the number of miles travelled and C is the total cost, in pounds.

C is the subject.

b) Work out the cost of a 5-mile journey.

$C = 6 + 2m$

$C = 6 + (2 \times 5)$ Substitute $m = 5$

$C = 6 + 10 = 16$

The fare is £16.

c) Charlie's taxi fare was £12. Work out the distance she travelled.

$C = 6 + 2m$ Substitute the known values.

$12 = 6 + 2m$ Alternatively, you can rearrange the formula to solve for m first.

$6 = 2m$ Subtract 6 from both sides.

$m = 6 \div 2 = 3$

The taxi travelled 3 miles.

> Don't forget to include units in your answer.

Rearranging a formula to change the subject

You will often want to find the value of a variable that is not the subject of the formula.

To change the subject of a formula, use inverse operations to isolate the subject.

> An exam question may ask you to rearrange a formula to make a different variable the subject.

a) Rearrange to make x the subject of $y = 3x + 2$.

$y - 2 = 3x$ Subtract 2 from both sides.

$\frac{y - 2}{3} = x$ Divide both sides by 3.

$x = \frac{y - 2}{3}$

b) Rearrange to make x the subject of $y = \frac{x + 3}{5}$

$5y = x + 3$ Multiply both sides by 5.

$5y - 3 = x$ Subtract 3 from both sides.

$x = 5y - 3$

c) i) Rearrange to make K the subject of $J = 3K^2$.

$J = 3K^2$

$\frac{J}{3} = K^2$ Divide both sides by 3.

$\sqrt{\frac{J}{3}} = K$ Take the square root of both sides.

ii) Work out the value of K when $J = 27$.

$\sqrt{\frac{27}{3}} = K$ Substitute the value of 27 for J.

$\sqrt{9} = K$ Remember a square root can be either positive or negative.

$K = \pm 3$

② Formulae

Using and writing formulae

1 A plumber charges a call-out fee of £130 plus an hourly rate of £65.

 a) Write a formula for the amount the plumber charges in total.

 ....

 b) Work out how much the plumber charges for a 4-hour job.

 £ ....

2 Mr Hussain buys pens and pencils at a shop. A box of pens, *a*, costs £3 and a box of pencils, *b*, costs £2.

 a) Write a formula to work out the total cost in pounds of buying the pens and pencils.

 ....

 b) Work out the total cost of 4 boxes of pens and 5 boxes of pencils.

 £ ....

Rearranging a formula to change the subject

3 The formula for calculating the area of a trapezium is $A = \frac{1}{2}(a + b)h$

 a) Rearrange the formula to make *b* the subject.

 ....

 b) This trapezium has an area of 78 cm². Work out the length *b*.

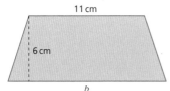

 11 cm

 6 cm

 b

 b = ... cm

② Straight–line graphs

Drawing straight-line graphs and the midpoint of a line segment

A **linear** graph is a straight-line graph, e.g. $y = x$, $y = 2x + 3$, $x + y = 5$.

To draw a linear graph:

1. Choose at least three values for x in the range of the graph. The points where $x = 0$ and $y = 0$ are often convenient to use.
2. Plot the points.
3. Connect the points with a straight line.

Complete the table of values for $y = 2x + 3$.

x	−2	−1	0	1	2
y	−1				7

When $x = -1$, $y = (2 \times -1) + 3 = 1$
When $x = 0$, $y = (2 \times 0) + 3 = 3$
When $x = 1$, $y = (2 \times 1) + 3 = 5$

> Work out each corresponding y value.

x	−2	−1	0	1	2
y	−1	1	3	5	7

> The table gives the points to plot on a graph: (−2, −1), (−1, 1), (0, 3), (1, 5) and (2, 7).

Draw the graph of $x + y = 5$ for values of x from 0 to 5.

Choosing $x = 0$, $x = 2$ and $x = 5$

> Choose three values for x.

When $x = 0$, $y = 5$
When $x = 2$, $y = 3$
When $x = 5$, $y = 0$

> Work out each corresponding y value.

x	0	2	5
y	5	3	0

> This gives the points to plot on the grid: (0, 5), (2, 3) and (5, 0).

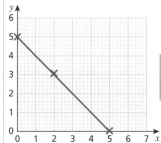

> Draw a straight, ruled line through the points.

Work out the midpoint of the line segment between (3, 2) and (−1, 4).

Midpoint $= (\frac{x_1 + x_2}{2}, \frac{y_1 + y_2}{2})$ Substitute the values of x and y.
$= (\frac{3 + (-1)}{2}, \frac{2 + 4}{2}) = (1, 3)$

Gradients

The **gradient** of a line is a measure of how steep the line is. A line going upwards from left-to-right has a **positive gradient** while a line going downwards has a **negative gradient**.

> To find an equation from a line, use two points to work out the gradient, then use the y-intercept to write the equation in the form $y = mx + c$.

To work out the gradient:

1. Find the coordinates of two points on the line.
2. Substitute them into the formula:

Gradient $= \frac{\text{Difference in } y \text{ values}}{\text{Difference in } x \text{ values}}$

You can draw triangles under the lines to help you.

> When finding the difference in the x and y values, remember to subtract the first x value from the second x value and the first y value from the second y value, or vice-versa.

Work out the gradient of these straight lines.

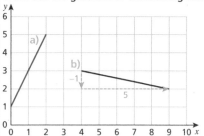

Two points on line a) are (0, 1) and (2, 5).

Gradient $= \frac{\text{Difference in } y \text{ values}}{\text{Difference in } x \text{ values}} = \frac{5 - 1}{2 - 0} = \frac{4}{2} = 2$

Two points on line b) are (4, 3) and (9, 2).

Gradient $= \frac{\text{Difference in } y \text{ values}}{\text{Difference in } x \text{ values}} = \frac{2 - 3}{9 - 4} = -\frac{1}{5}$

> The line slopes downwards from left to right, so the gradient is negative.

② Straight-line graphs

Drawing straight-line graphs and the midpoint of a line segment

1 Draw the graphs of:

a) $y = 3x - 3$ for values from $x = 0$ to $x = 4$

b) $2x + y = 6$ for values from $x = -1$ to $x = 3$

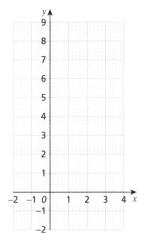

Gradients

2 Work out the gradients of the lines shown.

a)

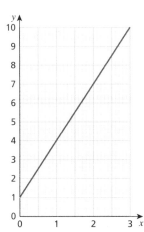

b)

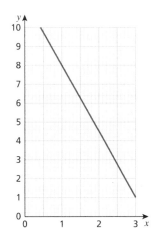

Gradient = ...

Gradient = ...

2 Quadratic graphs

Features of a quadratic graph

A **quadratic function** is one where the highest power of x is 2, e.g. $y = x^2 + 4x + 3$.

The graph of a **quadratic function** is a U-shaped **curve** called a parabola. The curve can open upwards $\smile$ or downwards $\frown$.

- The point at which the curve intersects the y-axis is the y-intercept. There will always be one and only one y-intercept.
- The point(s) at which the curve intersects the x-axis are the x-intercepts, also called the **roots**. There can be two, one or no x-intercepts.
- The roots are the solution to the quadratic equation when set equal to 0, e.g. $0 = x^2 + 4x + 3$.
- The **turning point** is the point at which the graph changes from increasing to decreasing or vice-versa. It is the top or bottom of the 'U' shape.

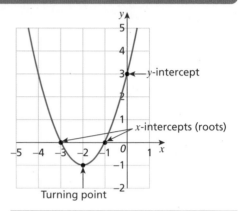

The graph of a quadratic equation is a $\smile$ or $\frown$ shape.

Plotting quadratic graphs

To draw a quadratic graph:
1. Complete a table of values.
2. Plot the points and draw a smooth curve.

Draw the graph of $y = x^2$ for values of x from −3 to 3.

x	−3	−2	−1	0	1	2	3
y	9	4	1	0	1	4	9

$y = x^2$

Plot the points (−3, 9), (−2, 4), and so on.

Draw a smooth curve through the points.

a) Draw the graph of $y = 2x^2 - x - 3$ for values of x from −1 to 2.

x	−1	0	1	2
$2x^2$	2	0	2	8
$-x$	1	0	−1	−2
-3	−3	−3	−3	−3
y	0	−3	−2	3

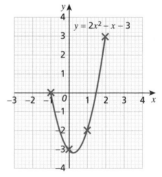

$y = 2x^2 - x - 3$

b) Use the graph to solve $2x^2 - x - 3 = 0$

$x = -1$ and $x = 1.5$

Read off at the points where $y = 0$ intersects the curve.

2) Quadratic graphs

Features of a quadratic graph

1 On the graph below, write down the coordinates of the:

a) y-intercept ....

b) x-intercept(s) ....

c) turning point. ....

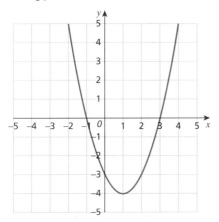

Plotting quadratic graphs

2 Plot the graph of $y = 2x^2 + 8x + 6$ for values of x from -4 to 0.

x	-4	-3	-2	-1	0
$2x^2$					
$8x$					
6					
y					

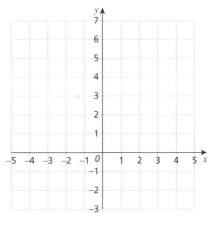

2 Cubic and reciprocal functions

Cubic functions

Cubic functions have an x^3 term as the highest power of x, e.g. $y = x^3$ or $y = x^3 - 4$.

Cubic functions may be given in factorised or partly factorised form, e.g. $y = x(x + 3)(x - 2)$.

The general form of a cubic function is given as $y = ax^3 + bx^2 + cx + d$ where a, b and c are coefficients and d is a constant.

The general shape of a cubic function is:

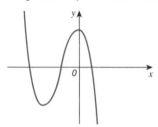

The general shape of a cubic function is an 'S' shaped curve. It can intersect the x-axis once, twice or three times.

Draw the graph of $y = x^3 - 2$ for values of x from −2 to 2.

Substitute the x values into the equation, e.g. $y = (-2)^3 - 2 = -8 - 2 = -10$

x	−2	−1	0	1	2
y	−10	−3	−2	−1	6

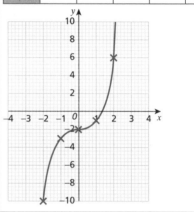

Reciprocal functions

Reciprocal functions are of the form $y = \frac{k}{x}$ where $x \neq 0$.

Make sure you know the general shape of a reciprocal function. The branches of the curve never reach the axes.

To graph reciprocal functions:
1. Fill in a table of values.
2. Plot the points and connect them with a smooth curve.

Draw the graph of $y = \frac{1}{x}$ for $x \neq 0$.

x	y
−4	$-\frac{1}{4}$
−3	$-\frac{1}{3}$
−2	$-\frac{1}{2}$
−1	−1
1	1
2	$\frac{1}{2}$
3	$\frac{1}{3}$
4	$\frac{1}{4}$

There are no values for $x = 0$ in a reciprocal function as you can't divide by zero.

Substitute the values of x, e.g. when $x = 4$, $y = \frac{1}{4}$

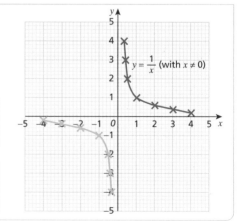

2 Cubic and reciprocal functions

Cubic functions

1 Complete the table of values and draw the graph of $y = x^3 + 1$.

x	−2	−1	0	1	2
y					

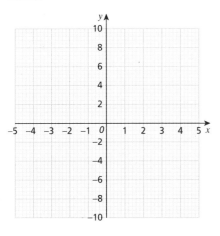

Reciprocal functions

2 Complete the table of values and draw the graph of $y = \frac{3}{x}$

x	−3	−2	−1	1	2	3
y						

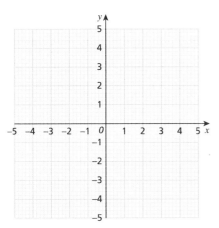

2) Real-life graphs

Distance-time graphs

You can use a distance–time graph to:

- find the distance travelled in a given time
- work out the average speed of a journey:

  average speed = $\frac{\text{distance travelled}}{\text{time taken}}$

- find which part of a journey is faster.

The steeper a line is on the graph, the faster the journey. A horizontal line means there is no movement (the journey has stopped).

> On a distance-time graph, the y-intercept represents the starting value and the gradient is the speed.

The graph shows Sara's journey home from school. She stopped at the library on the way.

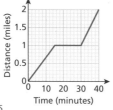

a) How long did she stop at the library?

30 − 15 = 15 minutes

> The line is horizontal between 15 and 30 minutes.

b) Work out her average speed from school to the library in miles per hour.

She travels 1 mile in 15 minutes.

Average speed = $\frac{\text{distance travelled}}{\text{time taken}}$

$= 1 \div \frac{1}{4}$

$= 4$ mph ← 15 minutes = $\frac{1}{4}$ hour

c) What is the distance from school to home?

Home is 2 miles from school.

Other graphs in context

Gradients show the rate of change. A steeper line (a bigger gradient) has a faster rate of change.

> / means the rate is increasing.
> \ means the rate is decreasing.

Here is a time series graph showing the growth of a sunflower over 28 days.

Approximately how tall was the sunflower on day 10?

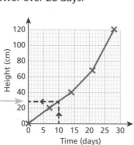

> Draw a line from 10 on the horizontal axis to the graph, then follow it over to the vertical axis. Note the scale on the y-axis.

The sunflower was approximately 28 cm tall.

Use the conversion graph to work out how many kilometres are in 15 miles.

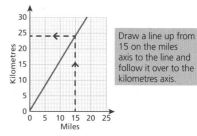

> Draw a line up from 15 on the miles axis to the line and follow it over to the kilometres axis.

15 miles is approximately 24 km.

This container is being filled with water. Sketch a graph showing the depth of water in the container over time.

> The container is narrower at the bottom so fills faster at first, then gets slower towards the middle before getting faster again. The sides of the container are not vertical, so the line is curved.

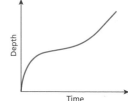

② Real-life graphs

Distance-time graphs

1 The graph shows Abdul's journey to two shops and back home.

a) For how long did Abdul stop in the two shops in total?

.... minutes

b) What was Abdul's average speed on the way home from the shops?

.... mph

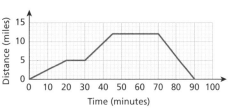

Other graphs in context

2 Four containers are filled with water.

Draw lines to match each container with the sketch showing the depth of water as it is filled.

a)   b)   c)   d)

1   2   3   4

3 This graph shows the historical population of a town.

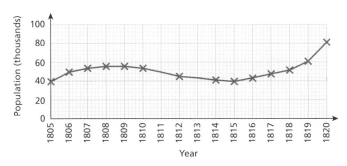

a) Between which **two** years was the population growth the fastest?

.... and ....

b) In which year was the population the same as it was in 1805?

....

2 Solving linear equations

Multi-step equations

To solve equations, use inverse operations to isolate the variable.

> Whatever you do to one side of the equation, you must also do to the other side.

a) Solve $2x + 3 = 11$

$$2x \boxed{\begin{matrix}+3\\-3\end{matrix}} = 11 \\ -3$$

$$2x = 8$$
$$\frac{2x}{2} = \frac{8}{2}$$
$$x = 4$$

Subtract 3 from both sides of the equation to leave just the x term on the left-hand side. Note that $+3$ and -3 give a zero, shown by the circle.

Divide both sides by 2 to leave just x on the left-hand side.

b) Solve $8x - 5 = 4x + 3$

$$8x \boxed{\begin{matrix}-5\\+5\end{matrix}} = 4x + 3 \\ +5$$

$$8x = \boxed{4x} + 8$$
$$-4x \boxed{-4x}$$

$$4x = 8$$
$$\frac{4x}{4} = \frac{8}{4}$$
$$x = 2$$

Add 5 to both sides of the equation to leave just the x term on the left-hand side. Note that -5 and $+5$ give a zero, shown by the circle.

Subtract $4x$ from both sides of the equation to leave just the number 8 on the right-hand side.

Divide both sides by 4 to leave just x on the left-hand side.

Linear equations with brackets

To solve equations with brackets, first expand the brackets, then solve.

Solve $6(2x - 1) = 5(2x + 4)$

$$12x - 6 = 10x + 20$$
$$12x \boxed{\begin{matrix}-6\\+6\end{matrix}} = 10x + 20 \\ +6$$

$$12x = \boxed{10x} + 26$$
$$-10x \boxed{-10x}$$

$$2x = 26$$
$$\frac{2x}{2} = \frac{26}{2}$$
$$x = 13$$

Multiply out the brackets on both sides.

Add 6 to both sides of the equation to leave just the x term on the left-hand side.

Subtract $10x$ from both sides of the equation to leave just the number 26 on the right-hand side.

Divide both sides by 2 to leave just x on the left-hand side.

② Solving linear equations

Multi-step equations

1 Solve each equation.

a) $3x - 8 = 4$

b) $5x - 2 = 3x + 4$

$x = $ ....

$x = $ ....

c) $3x - 12 = x - 4$

d) $18 = 6 - 3x$

$x = $ ....

$x = $ ....

Linear equations with brackets

2 Solve each equation.

a) $3(x - 4) = 2x - 15$

b) $2(3x + 4) = 2(4x - 1)$

$x = $ ....

$x = $ ....

c) $2(x - 3) = 9 - x$

d) $3(x - 1) = 2(2x - 5)$

$x = $ ....

$x = $ ....

2 Solving quadratic equations

Quadratic equations of the form $x^2 + bx + c = 0$

To solve a quadratic equation by factorising:

1. Rearrange the equation to the form
   $x^2 + bx + c = 0$
2. Factorise $x^2 + bx + c$
3. Set each bracket equal to zero.
4. Solve the linear equations.

Since the product of the brackets is equal to zero, one of the brackets must be equal to zero.

> **To solve after factorising, set each bracket equal to zero and solve for x.**

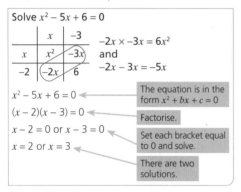

Solve $x^2 - 5x + 6 = 0$

	x	-3
x	x^2	$-3x$
-2	$-2x$	6

$-2x \times -3x = 6x^2$
and
$-2x - 3x = -5x$

$x^2 - 5x + 6 = 0$ — The equation is in the form $x^2 + bx + c = 0$

$(x - 2)(x - 3) = 0$ — Factorise.

$x - 2 = 0$ or $x - 3 = 0$ — Set each bracket equal to 0 and solve.

$x = 2$ or $x = 3$ — There are two solutions.

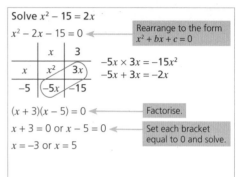

Solve $x^2 - 15 = 2x$

$x^2 - 2x - 15 = 0$ — Rearrange to the form $x^2 + bx + c = 0$

	x	3
x	x^2	$3x$
-5	$-5x$	-15

$-5x \times 3x = -15x^2$
$-5x + 3x = -2x$

$(x + 3)(x - 5) = 0$ — Factorise.

$x + 3 = 0$ or $x - 5 = 0$ — Set each bracket equal to 0 and solve.

$x = -3$ or $x = 5$

If a quadratic equation does not have a bx term, you can simply solve and take the square root.

> **A quadratic equation can have 0, 1 or 2 solutions.**

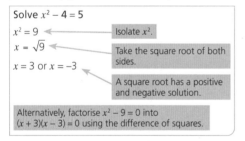

Solve $x^2 - 4 = 5$

$x^2 = 9$ — Isolate x^2.

$x = \sqrt{9}$ — Take the square root of both sides.

$x = 3$ or $x = -3$ — A square root has a positive and negative solution.

Alternatively, factorise $x^2 - 9 = 0$ into
$(x + 3)(x - 3) = 0$ using the difference of squares.

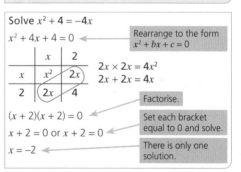

Solve $x^2 + 4 = -4x$

$x^2 + 4x + 4 = 0$ — Rearrange to the form $x^2 + bx + c = 0$

	x	2
x	x^2	$2x$
2	$2x$	4

$2x \times 2x = 4x^2$
$2x + 2x = 4x$

Factorise.

$(x + 2)(x + 2) = 0$

$x + 2 = 0$ or $x + 2 = 0$ — Set each bracket equal to 0 and solve.

$x = -2$ — There is only one solution.

Reasoning and problem solving with quadratic equations

An exam question that tests problem solving skills will sometimes require you to solve a quadratic equation.

The solutions of a quadratic equation are $x = 2$ and $x = -4$.	$x = 2$ and $x = -4$	Set up the linear equations.
	So $x - 2 = 0$ or $x + 4 = 0$	
Work out the equation.	So $(x - 2)(x + 4) = 0$	Combine the equations to form a quadratic.
To obtain the quadratic equation, work backwards from the solutions.	$x^2 + 2x - 8 = 0$	Expand the brackets.

2 Solving quadratic equations

Quadratic equations of the form $x^2 + bx + c = 0$

1 Solve each equation.

   a) $x^2 - 5x - 24 = 0$

$x =$ ....

   b) $x^2 = 15 - 2x$

$x =$ ....

   c) $x^2 - 10x = -16$

$x =$ ....

Reasoning and problem solving with quadratic equations

2 Given the solutions to the quadratic equations, work out the equations in the form $x^2 + bx + c = 0$

   a) $x = 4$ and $x = -5$

   b) $x = 3$

② Simultaneous equations

Solving by substitution and elimination

To solve a pair of simultaneous equations means to find a solution that works for both equations.

To solve by substitution:
1. Rearrange one equation into the form $y = ...$ or $x = ...$
2. Substitute for y or x in the other equation.
3. Solve the equation in the remaining variable.
4. Substitute this value back into the rearranged equation and solve.
5. Check that your solutions satisfy both of the original equations.

> Substitution is a good method to use if the coefficient of one of the variables is 1.

To solve by elimination:
1. Multiply one or both of the equations to match the coefficient of one of the variables.
2. Eliminate this variable by adding or subtracting the equations.
3. Solve the linear equation of the remaining variable.
4. Substitute this value back into one of the original equations and solve.
5. Check that your solutions satisfy both of the original equations.

> If the signs on the coefficient are the same, subtract one equation from the other. If the signs are different, add the equations.

Solve the simultaneous equations
$3x + 2y = 7$ and $x - y = -1$.

$3x + 2y = 7$ (1) — Number the equations (1) and (2) to keep track of your workings.

$x - y = -1$ (2)

$x - y = -1$ (2) — Rearrange equation (2) into the form $x = ...$

$x = -1 + y$ (3)

$3(-1 + y) + 2y = 7$ — Substitute equation (3) for x in equation (1).

$-3 + 3y + 2y = 7$

$5y = 10$, so $y = 2$

$x = -1 + y$

$x = -1 + 2$, so $x = 1$ — Substitute $y = 2$ into one of the equations and solve.

Solutions are $x = 1$ and $y = 2$

Substitute the values of x and y into the original equations and check they work.

Check: $3x + 2y = 7$ $3 + 4 = 7$ ✓
           $x - y = -1$ $1 - 2 = -1$ ✓

Solve the simultaneous equations
$2x + 4y = 2$ and $3x + 2y = 7$.

$2x + 4y = 2$ (1)

$3x + 2y = 7$ (2)

$6x + 4y = 14$ (3) — Multiply equation (2) by 2 to get the coefficient of y to be 4.

$6x + 4y = 14$
$- (2x + 4y = 2)$ — Line up the terms and subtract equation (1) from equation (3) to eliminate the y term.
$\overline{ 4x = 12}$
$ x = 3$

$2x + 4y = 2$

$(2 \times 3) + 4y = 2$ — Substitute $x = 3$ into equation (1) and then solve.

$6 + 4y = 2$

$4y = -4$, so $y = -1$

Solutions are $x = 3$ and $y = -1$

Check: $2x + 4y = 2$ $6 - 4 = 2$ ✓
           $3x + 2y = 7$ $9 - 2 = 7$ ✓

Solving simultaneous equations graphically

To solve simultaneous equations graphically:
1. Draw the graphs of both equations.
2. Find the points of intersection (or estimate them if they do not intersect at an exact point) – those are the solutions.

Solve $x + y = 5$ and $2x + y = 7$.

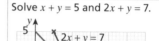
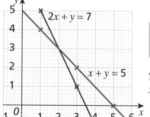

Point of intersection is (2, 3).

Solutions are $x = 2$ and $y = 3$

2 Simultaneous equations

Solving by substitution and elimination

1 Solve the following pairs of simultaneous equations.

a) $4x - y = 1$ and $y + 3 = 2x$

$x = \text{...................}, y = \text{...................}$

b) $2x + 3y = 9$ and $4x - 9y = 3$

$x = \text{...................}, y = \text{...................}$

Solving simultaneous equations graphically

2 Write down approximate solutions to the simultaneous equations $x - 4y = 5$ and $2x + y = 2$

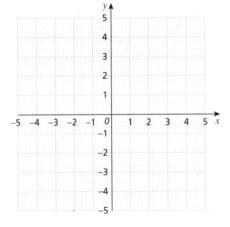

$x = \text{...................}, y = \text{...................}$

② Writing and solving equations in context

Linear equations

You will need to write and solve linear equations in a variety of contexts, such as in geometrical problems or when using rates of change.

> Writing a linear equation often involves simplifying more than one term and solving the equation in context.

A plumber charges a call-out fee of £50 plus £80 per hour.

a) Write an equation to work out the total cost of hiring the plumber.

$T = 50 + 80x$ where x is the number of hours and T is the total cost, in pounds.

b) The plumber takes 3 hours to do a job. Work out the total cost.

$T = 50 + (80 \times 3)$ ← Substitute $x = 3$
$\quad = 50 + 240 = £290$

c) The plumber charges £730 for a job. How long did the job take?

$730 = 50 + 80x$
$680 = 80x$ ← Subtract 50 from both sides.
$x = 680 \div 80 = 8.5$ ← Divide both sides by 80.
The job took 8.5 hours.

Here is an isosceles triangle, ABC.

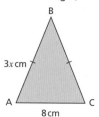

a) Write an equation for the perimeter of the triangle.

$P = 3x + 3x + 8$ ← Add up all the sides.
$P = (6x + 8)$ cm

b) The perimeter is 32 cm. Work out the value of x.

$6x + 8 = 32$ ← Substitute $P = 32$
$6x = 24$ ← Subtract 8 from both sides.
$x = 4$ ← Divide both sides by 6.

c) Work out the length of each side.

Given $x = 4$, then $3x = 3 \times 4 = 12$
The sides are 12 cm, 12 cm and 8 cm.

Quadratic equations

An area problem may require you to solve a quadratic equation.

Here is a rectangular garden.

$(x + 3)$ m

$(x + 2)$ m

a) Write an equation for its area. Give your answer in expanded form.

$A = (x + 2)(x + 3)$ ← $A = l \times w$
$A = x^2 + 2x + 3x + 6$ ← Expand the brackets.
$A = x^2 + 5x + 6$ ← Simplify.

b) The area of the garden is 90 m². Work out the value of x.

$x^2 + 5x + 6 = 90$ ← Substitute $A = 90$
$x^2 + 5x - 84 = 0$ ← Rearrange.
$(x + 12)(x - 7) = 0$ ← Factorise.
$x + 12 = 0$ or $x - 7 = 0$
$x = -12$ or $x = 7$ ← Set brackets to equal 0.

x cannot be -12 because the dimensions would be negative (if $x = -12$, then $x + 3 = -12 + 3 = -9$).

x must be 7.

c) Work out the dimensions of the garden.

Given $x = 7$, then $x + 2 = 7 + 2 = 9$ and
$x + 3 = 7 + 3 = 10$ ← Substitute $x = 7$ into each length.
9 m by 10 m

2 Writing and solving equations in context

Linear equations

1 Here is a triangle.

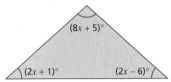

a) Write an equation for the sum of the angles in the triangle.

....

b) Use your answer to part a) to work out the value of x.

$x =$ ....

c) Work out the size of each angle in the triangle.

.... °, ... ° and .... °.

Quadratic equations

2 Here is a parallelogram.

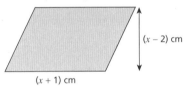

$(x - 2)$ cm

$(x + 1)$ cm

a) Write an equation in terms of x for the area of the parallelogram.

....

b) The area of the parallelogram is 70 cm².

Work out the value of x.

$x =$ ....

c) Work out the dimensions of each side.

.... cm and .... cm

Algebra **53**

② Solving inequalities

Inequalities on a number line

Inequalities use the symbols:

$<$ to mean 'less than'

$>$ to mean 'greater than'

$\leqslant$ to mean 'less than or equal to'

$\geqslant$ to mean 'greater than or equal to'.

The solution to an inequality can be shown on a number line using open circles (O) and closed circles (●):

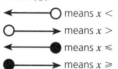

Show each of these inequalities on a number line.

a) $x < 1$

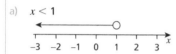

b) $x > 4$

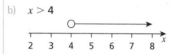

c) $x \leqslant 1$

d) $x \geqslant 4$

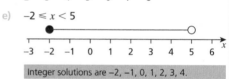

e) $-2 \leqslant x < 5$

Integer solutions are −2, −1, 0, 1, 2, 3, 4.

Make sure you know all the inequality symbols and understand the difference between them.

Solving inequalities

To solve a linear inequality:

1. Use the same techniques as when solving an equation.
2. Always collect terms so that the x term has a positive coefficient.
3. Rewrite the answer with x on the left-hand side if needed.

Keep the x term (or other variable) positive and never replace the inequality symbol with an equals sign.

a) Solve $3x - 3 \geqslant x + 7$

$3x - 3 \geqslant x + 7$ — Subtract x from both sides.
$2x - 3 \geqslant 7$ — Add 3 to both sides.
$2x \geqslant 10$ — Divide both sides by 2.
$x \geqslant 5$

b) Solve $-2x > 6$

$-2x > 6$ — Subtract 6 from both sides.
$-6 - 2x > 0$ — Add $2x$ to both sides.
$-6 > 2x$
$-3 > x$ or — If −3 is greater than x, then x is less than −3.
$x < -3$

c) Solve $6 < 3x \leqslant 12$

Split into two inequalities and solve.

$6 < 3x \leqslant 12$
$6 < 3x$ and $3x \leqslant 12$
$2 < x \qquad x \leqslant 4$

Divide through by 3.

$2 < x \leqslant 4$ — Write as a compound inequality.

3 and 4 are integer solutions that satisfy the inequality.

② Solving inequalities

Inequalities on a number line

1 Show each inequality on the number line.

a) $x < 2$

```
 ┬──┬──┬──┬──┬──┬──┬──┬──┬──→ x
-4 -3 -2 -1  0  1  2  3  4
```

b) $x \geqslant -1$

```
 ┬──┬──┬──┬──┬──┬──┬──┬──┬──→ x
-4 -3 -2 -1  0  1  2  3  4
```

c) $-2 < x \leqslant 3$

```
 ┬──┬──┬──┬──┬──┬──┬──┬──┬──→ x
-4 -3 -2 -1  0  1  2  3  4
```

Solving inequalities

2 Solve each inequality.

a) $3x + 2 < 8$

b) $-7 > 8 - 3x$

c) $2x + 1 \leqslant 3x + 2$

d) $15 < 5x \leqslant 20$

(2) Linear sequences

Vocabulary

A **sequence** is a set of numbers with a rule to find each number.

A **linear sequence** (or an **arithmetic sequence**) increases or decreases by the same amount from one term to the next.

A **term-to-term rule** is a rule that links one term to the next term.

The **nth term rule** (or **position-to-term rule**) links the position of the term to the value of the term.

The sequence of odd numbers is 1, 3, 5, 7, 9, ...

The term-to-term rule is: Start with 1 and add 2.

The position-to-term rule is: Double the position number and subtract 1 (so the nth term rule is $2n - 1$).

Position	1	2	3	4	5
Term	1	3	5	7	9

Using the nth term rule

The nth term rule can be used to find the value of any term in a sequence.

To find the value, substitute the term number for n in the nth term rule.

> You can use the nth term rule to find any term in the sequence.

Work out the 1st, 2nd, 3rd and 10th terms of the sequence with nth term rule $2n - 3$.

When $n = 1$: $(2 \times 1) - 3 = -1$
When $n = 2$: $(2 \times 2) - 3 = 1$
When $n = 3$: $(2 \times 3) - 3 = 3$
When $n = 10$: $(2 \times 10) - 3 = 17$

Working out the nth term rule

The nth term of a sequence is a formula for the position-to-term rule, e.g. the formula for the nth term for odd numbers would be $2n - 1$.

To work out the nth term rule:
1. Find the common difference between each term of the sequence.
2. Write down the times table of the common difference.
3. Compare the times table and the terms to work out which number to add or subtract to get the term.
4. Write down the nth term rule.

> A table can help to organise your workings.

Work out the nth term rule of the sequence 7, 10, 13, 16, 19, ...

The common difference is +3.

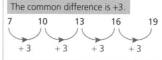

So the sequence is linked to the 3 times table.

Position	1	2	3	4	5
3 times table	3	6	9	12	15
	+4	+4	+4	+4	+4
Term	7	10	13	16	19

To get from the 3 times tables to the sequence, add 4.

To get from the position to the term, multiply the position by 3 then add 4.

The nth term rule is $3n + 4$.

Work out the nth term of this sequence:
11, 9, 7, 5, ...

The term-to-term rule is 'subtract 2'.

So the sequence is linked to the 2 times table.

So the nth term will be of the form $-2n + c$.
When $n = 1$: $\quad -2 \times 1 + c = 11$, so $c = 13$
So the nth term is $-2n + 13$ or $13 - 2n$.

② Linear sequences

Vocabulary

1 For each sequence, work out the term-to-term rule and the next **two** terms.

a) 2, 7, 12, 17, _____, _____

Term-to-term rule: _____

b) 12, 8, 4, 0, _____, _____

Term-to-term rule: _____

c) 9, 16, 23, 30, _____, _____

Term-to-term rule: _____

d) 56, 48, 40, _____, _____

Term-to-term rule: _____

Using the nth term rule

2 Work out the 1st, 2nd, 3rd and 10th term of the sequence with nth term rule $4n + 5$.

1st term: _____   2nd term: _____   3rd term: _____   10th term: _____

Working out the nth term rule

3 Work out the nth term for each sequence.

a) 5, 7, 9, 11, 13, …

b) 17, 14, 11, 8, …

2 Other sequences

Geometric sequences

In a **geometric sequence**, each term is multiplied by a **common ratio** to get the next term.

To find the common ratio, divide any two consecutive terms. It is a good idea to check a second set of consecutive terms.

a) Write the term-to-term rule for the sequence 2, 4, 8, 16, 32, ...

$4 \div 2 = 2$ ← Divide the second term by the first.
$8 \div 4 = 2$

The term-to-term rule is start at 2 and multiply by 2.

b) Work out the common ratio in the sequence 500, 100, 20, 4, ...

$100 \div 500 = \frac{1}{5}$ ← Divide the second term by the first.
$20 \div 100 = \frac{1}{5}$

The common ratio is $\frac{1}{5}$

c) Work out the missing term of the sequence 640, 160, 40, ___, 2.5

$160 \div 640 = \frac{1}{4}$ ← Find the common ratio.
$40 \div 160 = \frac{1}{4}$ ← Check with a second set of values.
$40 \times \frac{1}{4} = 10$

The missing term is 10. ← Multiply by the common ratio.

Other special number sequences

For square numbers, the nth term is n^2.

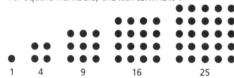

| 1 | 4 | 9 | 16 | 25 |

For cube numbers, the nth term is n^3.

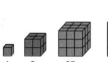

| 1 | 8 | 27 | 64 | 125 |

Triangular numbers can be represented like this:

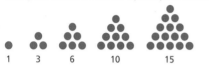

| 1 | 3 | 6 | 10 | 15 |

You may be asked to continue a sequence from pictures.

Square, cube and triangular numbers do not have a simple term-to-term rule.

a) Work out the next term in the sequence 3, 5, 8, 12, 17, ...

3   5   8   12   17

+2   +3   +4   +5

The sequence is increasing by +2, then +3, then +4, and so on.

The next term is $17 + 6 = 23$

b) The nth term rule of a sequence is $2n^2 - 3$.
Work out the first five terms.
When $n = 1$: $(2 \times 1^2) - 3 = -1$
When $n = 2$: $(2 \times 2^2) - 3 = 5$
When $n = 3$: $(2 \times 3^2) - 3 = 15$
When $n = 4$: $(2 \times 4^2) - 3 = 29$
When $n = 5$: $(2 \times 5^2) - 3 = 47$

Fibonacci-style sequences

In the Fibonacci sequence, each term is the sum of the two previous terms.

The Fibonacci sequence starts with 1 and 1.

The 3rd term is $1 + 1 = 2$ The 4th term is $1 + 2 = 3$

The 5th term is $2 + 3 = 5$ The 6th term is $3 + 5 = 8$

And so on.

Work out the next three terms in the Fibonacci-style sequence 3, 4, ...
The 1st missing term is: $3 + 4 = 7$
The 2nd missing term is: $4 + 7 = 11$
The 3rd missing term is: $7 + 11 = 18$

② Other sequences

Geometric sequences

1 Work out the common ratio of each sequence. Then work out the missing two terms.

a) 81, 27, 9, 3, ———, ———

Common ratio: ———

b) 3, 6, 12, 24, ———, ———

Common ratio: ———

c) 162, ———, ———, 6, 2

Common ratio: ———

Other special number sequences

2 Work out the next two terms in each sequence.

a) 4, 7, 12, 19, ———, ———

b) 20, 10, 2, −4, ———, ———

3 Work out the first three terms in the sequence with nth term rule $2n^3 + 5$.

Fibonacci-style sequences

4 Work out the next three terms in each Fibonacci-style sequence.

a) 2, 8, ———, ———, ———

b) −2, −4, ———, ———, ———

3 Converting units

Converting units of length

Units of length are mm, cm, m, km, and so on.

To convert between units of length:

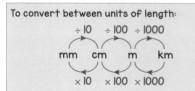

$\div 10 \quad \div 100 \quad \div 1000$

mm cm m km

$\times 10 \quad \times 100 \quad \times 1000$

A solar panel is 320 cm wide.
How wide is it in metres?

There are 100 cm in 1 m.

$320 \div 100 = 3.2$

The solar panel is 3.2 m wide.

Convert these measurements to centimetres.

a) 50 mm
50 mm = 5 cm ← $50 \div 10 = 5$

b) 1.3 m
1.3 m = 130 cm ← $1.3 \times 100 = 130$

c) 2 m 13 mm $\qquad$ $13 \div 10 = 1.3$
2 m = 200 cm and 13 mm = 1.3 cm
2 m 13 mm = 200 cm + 1.3 cm = 201.3 cm

Converting units of area

Units of area are units of length squared, e.g. mm², cm², m², and so on.

To convert between units of area:

$\div 10^2 \quad \div 100^2 \quad \div 1000^2$

mm² cm² m² km²

$\times 10^2 \quad \times 100^2 \quad \times 1000^2$

Convert these measurements to square centimetres.

a) 150 mm²
$150 \div 100 = 1.5$ cm² ← 10 mm = 1 cm, so divide by 10^2.

b) 1.5 m²
$1.5 \times 100^2 = 15000$ cm² ← 1 m = 100 cm, so multiply by 100^2.

A forest has an area of 4.23 km².
What is its area in square metres?

There are 1000 m in 1 km so multiply by 1000^2.

$4.23 \times 1000^2 = 4.23 \times 1000000 = 4230000$
The forest has an area of 4 230 000 m².

Converting units of volume

Units of volume are units of length cubed, e.g. mm³, cm³, m³, and so on.

Units of volume can also be given in ml, cl, l, and so on. In this case, convert between them in the same way as you do for lengths.

Note that 1 cm³ = 1 ml

To convert between units of volume:

$\div 10^3 \quad \div 100^3 \quad \div 1000^3$

mm³ cm³ m³ km³

$\times 10^3 \quad \times 100^3 \quad \times 1000^3$

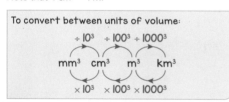

A metal drum holds 400 l of oil.

How many cubic metres does it hold?

There are 1000 ml in a litre.

400 l = 400 000 ml
400 000 ml = 400 000 cm³ ← 1 ml = 1 cm³
400 000 cm³ $\div 100^3 = 0.4$ m³

Converting units

Converting units of length

1 Convert these units to centimetres.

a) 13 m

.... cm

b) 130 mm

.... cm

2 A regular pentagon has side length 1.37 cm.

1.37 cm

Work out the side length in millimetres.

.... mm

Converting units of area

3 Convert these units to square centimetres.

a) 13 m²

.... cm²

b) 130 mm²

.... cm²

4 Loch Ness in Scotland has a surface area of 56.4 million square metres.

Work out the surface area in square kilometres.

.... km²

Converting units of volume

5 A cylinder has a volume of 35 000 cm³.

Work out the volume in cubic metres, giving your answer in standard form.

.... m³

③ Scale factors

Scale factors in shapes

A **scale factor** is a ratio between corresponding measurements that shows how much a length has been enlarged.

> In an enlarged shape, each side is multiplied by the same scale factor.

a) Shape B is an enlargement of shape A. Work out the scale factor.

Diagrams not drawn to scale

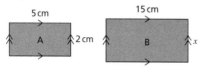

15 cm ÷ 5 cm = 3, so the scale factor is 3.

b) Work out the side length marked x.

3 × 2 cm = 6 cm

Line CD is three times the length of AB. The scale factor from line AB to line CD is 3.

Shape X is an enlargement of shape Y. Work out the scale factor.

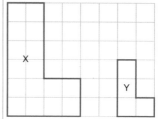

You are told it is an enlargement, so you only need to measure one side.

The base of the shape has changed from 4 units to 2 units, so the scale factor is 4 ÷ 2 = 2

Scale diagrams

To use a scale factor on a diagram:
1. Measure the desired length.
2. Multiply by the scale factor to find the actual length.

> Make sure you multiply by the scale factor.

Here is a floor plan of a kitchen drawn to a scale of 1 cm : 2 m.

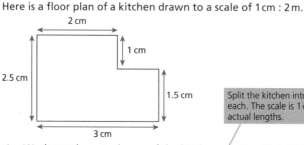

a) Work out the actual area of the kitchen floor in square metres.

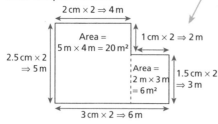

Total area = 20 m² + 6 m² = 26 m²

> Split the kitchen into two rectangles and find the area of each. The scale is 1 cm = 2 m, so multiply by 2 to find the actual lengths.

b) Abdul is laying new tiles on the kitchen floor. Tiles come in packs of 10 which cover a total of 2 m². Each pack costs £90.

Calculate the cost of the tiles he needs.

He needs 26 ÷ 2 = 13 packs of tiles
Total cost is 13 × £90.00 = £1170

③ Scale factors

Scale factors in shapes

1 Shape B is an enlargement of shape A.

Work out the scale factor. ....

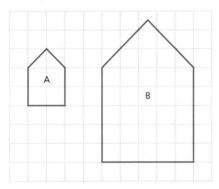

Scale diagrams

2 Here is a diagram of a lounge drawn to a scale of 2 units : 1 m.

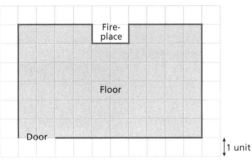

a) Work out the actual area of the floor in the lounge.

.... m²

b) Carpet is sold at a price of £14 per square metre.

How much will it cost to cover the floor with carpet?

£ ....

3 Ratio

Simplifying ratios

A **ratio** is used to compare two or more quantities and is written with a colon (:) between each value, e.g. the ratio of red to blue beads is 5 : 3.

To simplify a ratio means to write the ratio so that there are no common factors between the values.

> To simplify a ratio, divide all the parts by the same number until they cannot be divided any further.

Express 30 cm to 2 metres as a ratio in its simplest form.

30 cm : 2 metres = 30 cm : 200 cm

= 3 : 20

> When working with ratios, always use common units so they can cancel out.

The scale on a map is given as 1 cm to 2 km. Express this as a ratio in its simplest form.

1 km = 1000 metres; 1 metre = 100 cm

So 2 km = 200 000 cm ← Change to a common unit.

The ratio of the map is 1 cm : 200 000 cm

= 1 : 200 000 ← Cancel out the units.

Unit ratios

A **unit ratio** is written in the form 1 : n or n : 1. It can be used to compare ratios.

a) The ratio of cupcakes to biscuits at a party is 2 : 3. Write the ratio in the form 1 : n.

÷ 2 ⟋ 2 : 3 ⟍ ÷ 2

1 : 1.5

2 ÷ 2 = 1, so divide both sides by 2. This unit ratio means that for every one cupcake at the party, there are 1.5 biscuits.

b) At a small school, there are 173 students and 7 teachers. At a larger school, there are 550 students and 23 teachers. Which school has more students per teacher?

Write each ratio students : teacher in the form n : 1.

÷ 7 ⟋ 173 : 7 ⟍ ÷ 7
24.71 : 1

÷ 23 ⟋ 550 : 23 ⟍ ÷ 23
23.91 : 1

The smaller school has a larger number of students per teacher.

They are now both in the form n : 1 so you can compare them.

24.71 > 23.91, so the ratio of students to teachers is greater in the smaller school.

Ratios with decimals and fractions

Ratios can be written with decimals or fractions.

To simplify a ratio with a decimal:
1. Multiply all parts by the same value to make them integers.
2. Divide by the highest common factor.

> To simplify a ratio with a decimal or a fraction, first convert all the parts into integers.

Simplify 1.4 : 5

1.4 : 5

= 14 : 50

= 7 : 25 ← Simplify by dividing both sides by 2.

> Multiply both parts of the ratio by 10 so that you are working with integers.

To simplify a ratio with a fraction:
1. Write the fractions with a common denominator.
2. Multiply all the fractions by the common denominator.
3. Divide by the highest common factor.

Simplify $\frac{2}{3} : \frac{3}{4}$

$\frac{2}{3} = \frac{8}{12}$ and $\frac{3}{4} = \frac{9}{12}$ ← Write both fractions with a common denominator.

$\frac{8}{12} : \frac{9}{12}$

= 8 : 9 ← Multiply by the denominator.

③ Ratio

Simplifying ratios

1 Write each ratio in simplest form.

a) 3 : 12

b) 4 : 10

c) 2 cm : 1 km

d) 15 kg : 800 g

Unit ratios

2 Sara buys two bottles of squash which are both mixed with water to make a drink.
Bottle A requires 500 ml of squash and 1500 ml of water to make 2 litres of the drink.
Bottle B requires 160 ml of squash and 640 ml of water to make 800 ml of the drink.

a) Write the ratio of squash to water in each drink in the form n : 1.

Bottle A ....

Bottle B ....

b) Which bottle of squash requires a higher amount of squash per millilitre of water?

Ratios with decimals and fractions

3 Simplify the ratios.

a) 15 : 0.5

b) $\frac{2}{5} : \frac{4}{7}$

3 Further ratio

Dividing a quantity into a given ratio

You can share quantities into a given ratio. The parts in the ratio represent the proportions.

To divide into a given ratio:
1. Count the total parts of the ratio.
2. Divide the quantity by the total parts to find the value of one part.
3. Multiply by each part.

A drink is made of orange juice and water in the ratio 1 : 4.
How much water is used in a 200 ml drink?

$1 + 4 = 5$ parts in the ratio.

$200\,ml \div 5 = 40\,ml$ ←
$40\,ml \times 4 = 160\,ml$
160 ml of water in a 200 ml drink.

> Divide 200 ml by 5 parts to find the amount in 1 part of the ratio.

> Multiply to find the value of 4 parts in the ratio.

A paint is made by mixing blue, red and white paint in the ratio 3 : 2 : 2. A decorator needs 2.1 litres of paint. How much blue, red and white paint do they need?

$3 + 2 + 2 = 7$ parts in the ratio

2.1 litres = 2100 ml and
$2100\,ml \div 7 = 300\,ml$

> Divide 2.1 litres by 7 to find the amount in 1 part of the ratio.

Three parts is $300\,ml \times 3 = 900\,ml$
Two parts is $300\,ml \times 2 = 600\,ml$
The decorator needs 900 ml of blue, 600 ml of red and 600 ml of white paint.

Working out missing amounts in a ratio

You can find missing amounts in a ratio given the whole and part of the ratio.

To work out a missing amount in a ratio:
1. Divide the given amount by the given number of parts to find the value of one part.
2. Multiply the part corresponding to the unknown value by the result of step 1.

Currency exchange is a common context for ratio questions and in real life.

Given an exchange rate of £1 = another currency:
• To change from £ to the other currency, multiply by the exchange rate.
• To change from the other currency to £, divide by the exchange rate.

The ratio of adults to children at a football match is 7 : 3. There are 1500 children at the match. How many more adults are there than children?
There are 1500 children, so 3 parts = 1500
1 part = 500 ← Divide both sides by 3.
Adults represent 4 more parts than children.
1 part = 500, so 4 parts = 2000
There are 2000 more adults than children.

Meena is on holiday in France.
The exchange rate is £1 = €1.16
She buys a meal for €70.
How much does she spend in £?
€1.16 = £1
€70 = 70 ÷ 1.16 ← Divide by the exchange rate.
  = £60.34

Ratios as fractions

Matthew and Natasha share a pizza in the ratio 3 : 2.
What fraction does Matthew eat?

> Use the total number of parts in the ratio to represent the total number of pieces of pizza. Then write the number Matthew eats as a fraction of the total number of pieces.

The ratio has 5 parts altogether.
Matthew eats 3 out of the 5 parts, so he eats $\frac{3}{5}$ of the pizza.

When writing a ratio as a fraction, the denominator is the total number of parts in the ratio.

RETRIEVE

3 Further ratio

Dividing a quantity into a given ratio

1 Gary is raising money for charity. He will donate to charity X and charity Y in the ratio 2 : 3. He raises £1200.

How much does each charity receive?

Charity X = £ ....

Charity Y = £ ....

Working out missing amounts in a ratio

2 Katya is also raising money for charity. She donates to three charities (A, B and C) in the ratio 1 : 3 : 2. She donates £54 to charity B.

a) How much does she donate to charity A and charity C?

Charity A = £ ....

Charity C = £ ....

b) How much does she donate in total?

£ ....

Ratios as fractions

3 The ratio of adults to children at a cinema is 4 : 1.

a) Write the proportion of adults as a fraction of all the people at the cinema.

....

b) There are 120 people at the cinema.

How many of them are adults?

....

③ Proportion

Proportion calculations

A **proportion** is a comparison of a part to a whole. Two values are in **direct proportion** if the ratio between them remains fixed as the values change, e.g. the number of miles travelled when driving at a constant speed.

You can use the **unitary method** or **equivalence method** to solve problems in direct proportion.

To use the unitary method:
1. Write out the proportion.
2. Find the amount of one part of the whole.
3. Multiply to find the desired amount.

The unitary method works by finding the value of one unit. If the numbers work out nicely, the equivalence method may be easier.

To use the equivalence method:
1. Write out the proportion.
2. Write out the proportion you are trying to find.
3. Work out the multiplier (divide the bottom by the top).
4. Multiply the other side by the multiplier.

---

a) Here are some ingredients needed to make 12 biscuits:

Work out the amount of sugar needed to make 18 biscuits.

> 100 g butter
> 60 g sugar
> 120 g flour

Unitary method

$$\div 12 \left(\begin{array}{c} 60\,g = 12 \text{ biscuits} \\ 5\,g = 1 \text{ biscuit} \\ 90\,g = 18 \text{ biscuits} \end{array}\right) \div 12$$
$$\times 18 \qquad \qquad \times 18$$

Equivalence method

60 g = 12 biscuits   The proportion you are trying to find.
___ g = 18 biscuits

18 ÷ 12 = 1.5, so the multiplier is 1.5

$$\times 1.5 \left(\begin{array}{c} 60\,g = 12 \text{ biscuits} \\ 90\,g = 18 \text{ biscuits} \end{array}\right) \times 1.5$$

b) Two bags of flour cost £2.36. How much do three bags cost?

$$\div 2 \left(\begin{array}{c} 2 \text{ bags} = £2.36 \\ 1 \text{ bag} = £1.18 \\ 3 \text{ bags} = £3.54 \end{array}\right) \div 2$$
$$\times 3 \qquad \qquad \times 3$$

Value for money

A common application of proportions is working out the best value for money, or the best deal.

To compare value for money, work out the cost per unit or use the equivalence method.

A bottle of laundry detergent costs £9.00 for 50 washes.
A box of laundry capsules is on offer for £5.00 for 30 washes.
Which is the better deal?

Comparing the cost per wash

Bottle of detergent:

> Divide by 50 to find the cost of one wash.

$$\div 50 \left(\begin{array}{c} £9.00 = 50 \text{ washes} \\ 18p = 1 \text{ wash} \end{array}\right) \div 50$$

Alternatively, you could work out how much 30 washes would cost using the bottle of detergent or how much 50 washes would cost using the box of capsules.

Laundry capsules:

$$\div 30 \left(\begin{array}{c} £5.00 = 30 \text{ washes} \\ 16.67p = 1 \text{ wash} \end{array}\right) \div 30$$

The laundry capsules are a better deal as they cost less per wash.

③ Proportion

Proportion calculations

1 A recipe is shown for Yorkshire pudding to serve 4 people.

> **Yorkshire Pudding (serves 4 people)**
>
> 100 grams plain flour   200 ml milk
> 2 eggs   50 ml water

How much of each ingredient is needed to make Yorkshire pudding for 6 people?

a) Flour   **b)** Milk

.... g   .... ml

c) Eggs   **d)** Water

.... ml

Value for money

2 A 70 g bag of sweets costs £1.40
A 1 kg tub of sweets costs £10

Which is the better deal? Show your workings.

3 A 200 ml bottle of shampoo costs £6
A 500 ml bottle of shampoo costs £10

Which is the better deal? Show your workings.

③ Percentages

Fractions, decimals and percentages

A **percentage** (%) is an amount expressed as fraction of 100.

To convert from:
- a decimal to a percentage → multiply by 100
- a percentage to a decimal → divide by 100
- a fraction to a percentage → divide the numerator by the denominator, then multiply by 100 (if the denominator is a factor or multiple of 100, you can use equivalent fractions to write the fraction over 100)
- a percentage to a fraction → write the percentage as a fraction over 100, then simplify.

Percentage	Fraction	Decimal
50%	$\frac{1}{2}$	0.5
25%	$\frac{1}{4}$	0.25
75%	$\frac{3}{4}$	0.75
10%	$\frac{1}{10}$	0.1
$33\frac{1}{3}$%	$\frac{1}{3}$	0.333...
$66\frac{2}{3}$%	$\frac{2}{3}$	0.666...

Write 72% as a fraction in its simplest form.

72% means 72 out of 100.

$$72\% = \frac{72}{100} = \frac{18}{25}$$

÷4 ... ÷4

Convert $\frac{7}{20}$ to a percentage.

Method 1

$$\frac{7}{20} \times 100 = \frac{700}{20} = 35\%$$

Method 2

20 is a factor of 100, so you can use equivalent fractions.

$$\frac{7}{20} = \frac{35}{100} = 35\%$$

×5 ... ×5

Calculating percentages

To calculate a percentage of a quantity:
1. Change the percentage to a fraction or a decimal.
2. Multiply by the fraction or decimal.

Or
1. Break up the percentage into tens and ones.
2. Find 10%, 1% and 5% as needed.
3. Combine the amounts.

To find:
- 10% of a quantity, divide the quantity by 10.
- 5% of a quantity, divide 10% of the quantity by 2.
- 1% of a quantity, divide the quantity by 100.

Work out 82% of 200 grams.

Method 1

82% is $\frac{82}{100}$

$$\frac{82}{100} \times 200g = 164g$$

Method 2

10% of 200g is 200 ÷ 10 = 20

1% of 200g is 200 ÷ 100 = 2

Then 80% of 200g is 20 × 8 = 160 80% is 10% × 8

And 2% of 200g is 2 × 2 = 4 ← 2% is 1% × 2

So 82% of 200g is 160 + 4 = 164g

Writing one quantity as a percentage of another

To write one quantity as a percentage of another:
1. Make sure both quantities are in the same units.
2. Express the quantity as a fraction of the other quantity.
3. Convert the fraction to a percentage.

a) Express 50p as a percentage of £2.

£2 = 200p   Change pounds to pence.

$$\frac{50}{200} = \frac{25}{100} = 25\%$$ Write 50p as a fraction of 200p and convert.

b) What is 120cm as a percentage of 1.6m?

1.6m = 160cm $\frac{120}{160} = \frac{3}{4}$

$$\frac{3}{4} \times 100 = 75\%$$

③ Percentages

Fractions, decimals and percentages

1 Complete the table to show the equivalent percentages, fractions and decimals.

Percentage	Fraction	Decimal
20%		
		0.45
62%		
	$\frac{11}{20}$	
		0.12
	$\frac{3}{8}$	

Calculating percentages

2 Work out 30% of 600 grams.

.... g

3 Work out 15% of £80.

£ ....

Writing one quantity as a percentage of another

4 What is 265 m as a percentage of 26.5 km?

.... %

③ Percentage change

Working out percentage change

To work out the percentage change:
1. Work out the change, e.g. increase, decrease, profit or loss.
2. Use the formula

$$\text{percentage change} = \frac{\text{change}}{\text{original amount}} \times 100\%$$

Mr Smith bought a ring for £250 and sold it for £400. Work out his percentage profit.

$$\text{Percentage profit} = \frac{\text{profit}}{\text{original amount}} \times 100\%$$

£400 − £250 is £150 profit. $= \frac{150}{250} \times 100 = 60\%$

Increasing or decreasing by a percentage

To increase or decrease a quantity by a percentage, use one of these two methods:

Increase/decrease

Work out the increase and add it on.

Or Work out the decrease and subtract it.

Multiplier method
1. Write down the multiplier.
2. Multiply the original amount by the multiplier.

a) Increase £17 000 by 5%

Method 1

5% of £17 000 is $\frac{5}{100} \times 17\,000 = £850$

New amount is £17 000 + £850 = £17 850

Method 2 (Multiplier method)

5% extra is the same as 100% + 5% = 105%

105% is $\frac{105}{100} = 1.05$ ◄—— 1.05 is the multiplier.

105% of £17 000 is 1.05 × 17 000 = £17 850

b) A TV is on offer for 20% off its original price of £450. Work out the TV's new price.

Method 1

20% of 450 is $\frac{20}{100} \times 450 = 90$

The new price is £450 − £90 = £360

Method 2

A 20% decrease is the same as 100% − 20% = 80% of the original price

80% of 450 is 0.8 × £450 = £360

Working out the original amount

You can use inverse operations (also called 'reverse percentages') to find the original amount after a percentage change.

To work out the original amount:
1. Write down the multiplier.
2. Divide the final amount by the multiplier.

To find the new amount, multiply by the multiplier.
To find the original amount, divide by the multiplier.

A new car loses 18% of its value in one year. At the end of the year, it is valued at £12 300. Work out its value at the start of the year.

The car loses value so subtract the percentage from 100.

100% − 18% = 82%

82% = 0.82 ◄—— 0.82 is the multiplier.

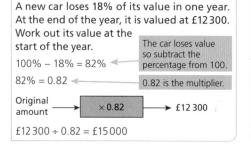

£12 300 ÷ 0.82 = £15 000

A company hires 12% more employees. It now has 728 employees. How many employees did the company have before?

100% + 12% = 112%

112% = 1.12 ◄—— 1.12 is the multiplier.

Original amount → ×1.12 → 728

728 ÷ 1.12 = 650

The company had 650 employees before.

Percentage change

Working out percentage change

1 The price of a shirt has been reduced from £15 to £12

What is the percentage reduction in the price?

.... %

Increasing or decreasing by a percentage

2 A bank account pays 3% interest per year. Kerry opens an account with £1200.

Work out the amount in her account at the end of the year.

£ ....

Working out the original amount

3 A builder charges £3000 for a job, including 20% VAT.

What is the cost of the job before VAT is added?

£ ....

4 A top is in a sale for 15% off the original price. The sale price is £21.25.

What was the original price?

£ ....

③ Compound units

Speed

A **compound measure** or **compound unit** is a measure of one quantity in relation to another. Speed is an example of a compound measure.

Speed is the distance travelled divided by the time taken. The units for speed are a distance (e.g. metres, kilometres, miles) per a unit of time (e.g. hours, minutes, seconds).

You can draw a formula triangle to help remember related formulae for compound measures.

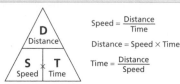

$Speed = \dfrac{Distance}{Time}$

$Distance = Speed \times Time$

$Time = \dfrac{Distance}{Speed}$

A cyclist completes a 231 km road race at an average speed of 44 km/h. What was their race time? Give your answer in hours and minutes.

Time = Distance ÷ Speed ← Use the formula triangle.

Time = 231 ÷ 44 = 5.25 = 5 hours and 15 minutes ← 0.25 hours = 60 × 0.25 = 15 minutes

Density and pressure

Density and pressure are also compound measures.

Density is a measure of a material's mass divided by its volume. The units are a measure of mass per unit of volume (e.g. g/cm^3).

Pressure is a measure of a force divided by the area to which the force is applied. The units are a measure of force per unit of area (e.g. N/m^2, where N is a Newton, a measure of force).

$Pressure = \dfrac{Force}{Area}$

$Force = Pressure \times Area$

$Area = \dfrac{Force}{Pressure}$

$Density = \dfrac{Mass}{Volume}$

$Mass = Density \times Volume$

$Volume = \dfrac{Mass}{Density}$

The air pressure inside a tyre is $220\,000\,N/m^2$. The area of tyre that touches the road is $0.005\,m^2$. Calculate the force applied by the tyre on the road.

Force = Pressure × Area ← Use the formula triangle.

Force = $220\,000\,N/m^2 \times 0.005\,m^2$

Force = 1100 N

A bronze ornament weighs 3.6 kg. Work out the volume of bronze used in the ornament given that the density of bronze is approximately $9\,g/cm^3$.

Volume = Mass ÷ Density

3.6 kg = 3600 g ← The density is given in grams.

Volume = $3600 ÷ 9 = 400\,cm^3$

Rates

A rate is a compound measure: something happens in a unit of time (e.g. the rate of water filling up a pool).

a) A hosepipe flows at a rate of 12 litres per minute as it fills up a 420-litre paddling pool. How long does it take to fill the pool?

Draw a formula triangle. The rate is the volume per minute.

Time = Volume ÷ Rate

Time = 420 l ÷ 12 l/min = 35 minutes

b) Petrol flows from a pump at a rate of 13 litres per minute. The pump takes 3 minutes to fill a petrol tank. What is the volume of the tank?

Volume = Rate × Time

Volume = 13 l/min × 3 min = 39 litres

③ Compound units

Speed

1 A car travels a distance of 140 km at an average speed of 40 km/h.

How long does the journey take?

.... h

2 An aeroplane departs at 11:05 and lands at 13:15. It flies at an average speed of 924 km/h.

How far has the aeroplane flown?

.... km

Density and pressure

3 Gold has a density of approximately 19 g/cm³.

What is the volume of a gold bar of mass 11 kg? Give your answer to the nearest cubic centimetre.

.... cm³

4 A kettlebell exerts a force of 60 N on the floor over an area of 0.012 m².

Calculate the pressure exerted by the kettlebell on the floor.

$$\text{Pressure} = \frac{\text{Force}}{\text{Area}}$$

.... N/m²

Rates

5 Sand falls through a three-minute egg timer at a rate of 0.6 g/s.

What is the mass of sand in the timer?

.... g

③ Direct and inverse proportion

Direct proportion

Two values are in **direct proportion** if the ratio between each pair of values is the same. For example, the amount of a sugar in a recipe has to double in order to make double the number of biscuits.

Direct proportion can be expressed as an equation, $y = kx$, where k is the **constant of proportionality**.

The graph of direct proportion is a straight line starting at the origin with a gradient of k.

Shown opposite is the graph of $y = 2x$. The gradient is k = 2, so every y value is twice the corresponding x value.

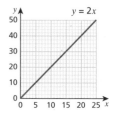

Proportionality can be shown using the symbol ∝ where $y \propto x$ means 'y is proportional to x'.

Show that this table of values is in direct proportion.

x	2	3	8	20
y	3	4.5	12	30

Find the ratio between each value.

x	2	3	8	20
y	3	4.5	12	30
y ÷ x	3 ÷ 2 = 1.5	4.5 ÷ 3 = 1.5	12 ÷ 8 = 1.5	30 ÷ 20 = 1.5

In each case $y \div x = 1.5$, so the values of x and y are in direct proportion.

Inverse proportion

Two values are **inversely proportional** if as one value increases, the other decreases at the same rate, e.g. as one doubles, the other halves.

y can also be inversely proportional to x^2, x^3, $\sqrt{x}$, and so on.

If two quantities y and x are inversely proportional, we write $y \propto \frac{1}{x}$ or $y = \frac{k}{x}$

A graph of inverse proportion is a **reciprocal** curve.

For all inverse proportion graphs, as x gets bigger, y gets smaller.

s is inversely proportional to t, with $s = \frac{30}{t}$. Complete the table.

t	60	10	15	
s				5

$s = \frac{30}{60} = \frac{1}{2}$ ← Substitute the values into the equation.

$s = \frac{30}{10} = 3$

$s = \frac{30}{15} = 2$

$5 = \frac{30}{t}$ ← Solve for t.

$5t = 30$

$t = 30 \div 5 \Rightarrow t = 6$

t	60	10	15	6
s	$\frac{1}{2}$	3	2	5

w is inversely proportional to v. Describe the effect on w when:

a) v is doubled

When v is doubled, w is halved.

b) v is halved

When v is halved, w is doubled.

c) v is multiplied by a scale factor of 0.3

When v is multiplied by 0.3, w is divided by 0.3

An aquarium has enough food to feed 150 zebrafish for 2 weeks. How long would the food last for 75 zebrafish?

The food available is inversely proportional to the number of fish.

75 is half of 150, so the food would last for double the length of time, which is 4 weeks.

Direct and inverse proportion

Direct proportion

1 y is directly proportional to x.

$y = 3x$

Work out the value of y when $x = 4$

$$y = \text{.........................}$$

2 A student made an error filling out a table of values where x is directly proportional to y.

Identify and correct the mistake.

x	2	4	5	8
y	8	12	20	32

Inverse proportion

3 y is inversely proportional to x.

$y = \frac{18}{x}$

Work out the value of y when $x = 4$

$$y = \text{.........................}$$

4 A printer has enough ink to last 3 weeks when it prints 600 pages a day.

How long will the ink last if 200 pages a day are printed?

.... weeks

③ Rates of change

Writing and interpreting rates of change in equations

A **rate of change** is a measure of how one value changes in relation to another.

> A straight line has a constant rate of change. A horizontal line means there is no change.

Write an equation to represent each scenario.

a) Car hire costs £40 per day. Write an equation showing the total cost for hiring a car for d days.

> It can help to write the equation in words.

Total cost = £40 × number of days

$T = 40d$ where T is the total cost and d is the number of days.

> Remember to say what the variables are.

b) A gardener charges £30 an hour plus a fixed travel cost of £20. Write an equation showing the total cost to hire the gardener for h hours.

> The £20 travel cost is constant; it is the same whatever the number of hours worked.

Total cost = (£30 × number of hours) + £20

$T = 30h + 20$ where T is the total cost and h is the number of hours.

Interpreting rates of change on straight-line graphs

On a straight-line graph, the gradient is the rate of change and the y-intercept is the initial value.

Rates of change can be compared by looking at the steepness of the lines.

The graph shows the total cost of hiring a pressure washer, including the delivery fee.

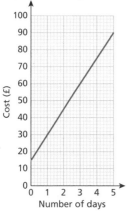

a) Write down the delivery fee.

The delivery fee is the y-intercept, £15.

b) Work out the cost per day to hire the pressure washer.

$\text{Gradient} = \frac{\text{change in } y}{\text{change in } x} = \frac{90 - 15}{5 - 0} = 15$

> (0, 15) and (5, 90) are two convenient points on the line for working out the change in y in relation to x.

It costs £15 per day to hire the pressure washer.

Ice is heated until it boils as water. The graph shows its temperature change.

At what rate does the temperature of the water increase from the ice melting to boiling point?

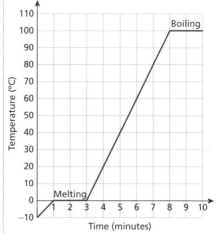

At melting point (0°C), the water begins to heat up at (3, 0). It begins to boil at (8, 100).

$\text{Gradient} = \frac{\text{change in } y}{\text{change in } x} = \frac{100 - 0}{8 - 3} = \frac{100}{5} = 20$

The temperature of the water increases by 20°C per minute.

> The steeper the straight line, the greater the rate of change.

Rates of change

Writing and interpreting rates of change in equations

1 Write equations to model each situation.

a) The number of steps taken when walking. Jai takes 2000 steps per mile when walking.

....

....

b) The value of a mobile phone that costs £500 when new. It decreases in value by £50 per year.

....

....

c) The total volume of water in a swimming pool being filled with a hosepipe that flows at 12 litres per minute.

....

....

Interpreting rates of change on straight-line graphs

2 The graph shows Paul's drive from home to work.

He stops at a coffee shop on the way.

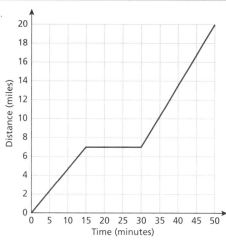

a) How far is the coffee shop from Paul's house?

.... miles

b) Does he drive faster from home to the coffee shop or from the coffee shop to work? Explain your answer.

....

....

c) How fast does Paul drive to work from the coffee shop?

.... mph

Exponential growth and decay

Compound interest and exponential growth

Simple interest means that the initial amount earns interest. **Compound interest** means the interest is earned on the balance in the account, including any previous interest earned.

Compound interest is an example of **exponential growth** because there is repeated percentage change.

Compound interest is best calculated using a multiplier.

Decreasing an amount by 10% is the same as finding 90% of the amount.

Increasing an amount by 10% is the same as finding 110% of the amount.

To increase an amount by r%, multiply by $1 + \frac{r}{100}$

To decrease an amount by r%, multiply by $1 - \frac{r}{100}$

$A = P\left(1 + \frac{r}{100}\right)^n$ where A is the amount after n increases, P is the initial amount, r is the rate of change and n is the number of increases.

To work out values of repeated percentage change:

1. Find the multiplier.
2. Substitute the given values into the formula $A = P\left(1 + \frac{r}{100}\right)^n$.
3. Work out the value needed.

£2000 is invested at 5% compound interest. Work out the value of the investment after 5 years.

Using a table

Number of years	Amount in account
0	£2000
1	£2000 × 1.05 = £2100
2	£2100 × 1.05 = £2205
3	£2205 × 1.05 = £2315.25
4	£2315.25 × 1.05 = £2431.01
5	£2431.01 × 1.05 = £2552.56

Using the formula $P = £2000$, $r = 0.05$ and $n = 5$

$A = P\left(1 + \frac{r}{100}\right)^n = 2000 \times 1.05^5 = £2552.56$

An ecologist is studying a population of tigers. She estimates that their numbers are increasing by 8% a year due to conservation efforts. If there are 175 tigers at the start of her study, estimate the tiger population after 5 years.

$8\% = 0.08$, then $1 + 0.08 = 1.08$ ← The population is increasing.

$A = P\left(1 + \frac{r}{100}\right)^n$

$A = 175 \times 1.08^5$ ← $P = 175$ and $n = 5$

$A = 257$ tigers

Exponential decay

Exponential decay occurs when a value decreases by a repeated percentage change.

Makers of a mobile phone estimate that the battery health decreases by 4% every 100 charge cycles. Calculate the battery health of a phone that has been through 500 charge cycles. Give your answer to the nearest percent.

$A = P\left(1 - \frac{r}{100}\right)^n$ ← The amount is decreasing.

$P = 100\%$ ← The initial amount is 100% battery health.

$r = 0.04$, so the multiplier is $1 - 0.04 = 0.96$

$n = 5$ ← The 4% loss is for every 100 charges, so $n = 5$ represents 500 charges.

$A = 100 \times 0.96^5 = 81.537... = 82\%$ battery health

3) Exponential growth and decay

Compound interest and exponential growth

1 £1500 is invested in a savings account that pays 3% compound interest.

Work out the amount in the account after 5 years.

£ ....

2 There are 25 foxes in a park. The population of foxes increases by 12% a year.

Calculate the expected number of foxes in the park after 3 years.

....

Exponential decay

3 A new computer costs £1200 and loses 16% of its value each year.

Calculate the value of the computer after 4 years.

£ ....

4 A new car costs £20 000 and loses 15% of its value each year.

Calculate the value of the car after 12 years.

£ ....

4 Constructions (1)

Constructing triangles

A construction is an accurate drawing made using a combination of a ruler, protractor and a pair of compasses.

> Leave all your construction marks and arcs in place. Don't rub them out.

You can **construct** a triangle if you know any of this information:
- the length of the three sides (SSS)
- the length of two sides and an angle between them (SAS)
- the size of two angles and a side between them (ASA).

> Remember SSS, SAS and ASA to construct triangles. These are the same criteria for congruent triangles.

a) Construct triangle ABC with AB = 3 cm, BC = 2.5 cm and AC = 2 cm

b) Construct triangle ABC with AB = 3 cm, AC = 2 cm and angle BAC = 70°

c) Construct triangle ABC with AB = 4 cm, angle BAC = 40° and angle ABC = 60°

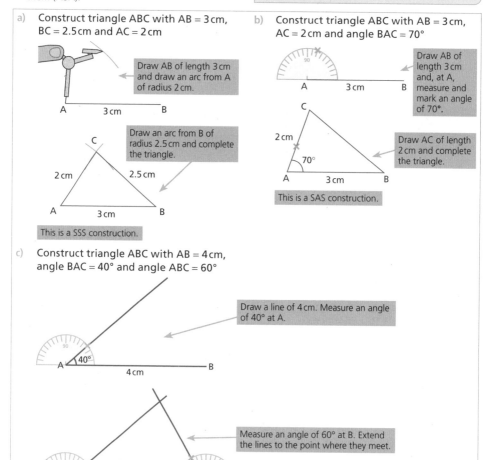

Draw AB of length 3 cm and draw an arc from A of radius 2 cm.

Draw an arc from B of radius 2.5 cm and complete the triangle.

This is a SSS construction.

Draw AB of length 3 cm and, at A, measure and mark an angle of 70°.

Draw AC of length 2 cm and complete the triangle.

This is a SAS construction.

Draw a line of 4 cm. Measure an angle of 40° at A.

Measure an angle of 60° at B. Extend the lines to the point where they meet.

This is an ASA construction.

4 Constructions (1)

Constructing triangles

1. Construct triangle ABC with side AB = 5 cm, side AC = 3 cm and angle CAB = 40°.

2. Construct triangle XYZ with side XZ = 7 cm, angle YXZ = 50° and angle YZX = 30°.

4 Constructions (2)

Constructing lines and angles

A **perpendicular** is a line drawn at right angles to another line. A **perpendicular bisector** is a line drawn at right angles to the midpoint of another line.

a) Draw a line AB. Construct the **perpendicular bisector** of the line AB.

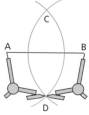
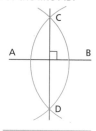

| Draw long arcs of equal radius from points A and B to intersect at points C and D. | Join C and D to form the perpendicular bisector. |

b) Draw a line AB. Construct a **perpendicular from a point O** to the line.

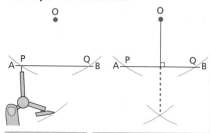

| Draw two arcs from O to cross AB at P and Q, then draw an arc from P. | Draw an arc from Q using the same radius as for the arc from P and complete the perpendicular. |

c) Construct a line **perpendicular to** PQ that passes through point A.

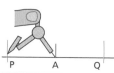
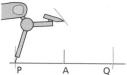
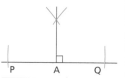

| Draw a line and mark a point A. Draw two equal arcs from A to cross the line. | Draw an arc from P of a longer radius than the two arcs already drawn. | Draw an arc from Q (same radius as that drawn from P) and complete the angle. |

You can construct these angles without a protractor:

- 90° by constructing a perpendicular to a point on a line
- 45° by bisecting a 90° angle
- 60° by following the steps to construct an equilateral triangle
- 30° by bisecting a 60° angle.

Use a ruler and a pair of compasses only to construct an angle of 60°.

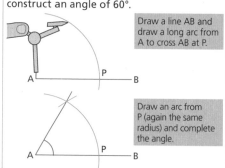

Draw a line AB and draw a long arc from A to cross AB at P.

Draw an arc from P (again the same radius) and complete the angle.

Construct the bisector of an angle.

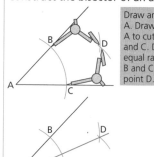

Draw an angle at point A. Draw a long arc from A to cut the lines at B and C. Draw arcs of equal radius from points B and C to intersect at point D.

Join A to D to form the bisector of the angle.

4 Constructions (2)

Constructing lines and angles

1 Construct the perpendicular bisector to line AB.

A —————————————————— B

2 Construct an angle of 45° on the line CD.

C —————————————————— D

4 Angles

Angle facts and angles in parallel lines

Angles **on a straight line** add up to **180°**.

Angles **at a point** add up to **360°**.

Vertically opposite angles are **equal**.

$a + c = 180°$
$b + c = 180°$
$b + d = 180°$
$a + d = 180°$

$a + b + c + d = 360°$

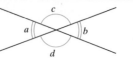

$a = b$
$c = d$

Alternate angles are equal.

In the exam, don't refer to alternate angles as 'Z' angles.

Corresponding angles are equal.

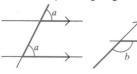

In the exam, don't refer to corresponding angles as 'F' angles.

Allied (co-interior) angles sum to 180°.

Work out the size of angle x.

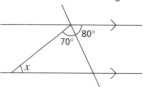

Because there are parallel lines, look out for any alternate or corresponding angles.

Method 1

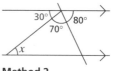

The missing angle on the straight line is 30°.

x and 30° are alternate angles, so $x = 30°$

Method 2

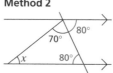

The other angle in the triangle is alternate to 80°.

Angles in a triangle add up to 180°, so x is
$180° - 70° - 80° = 30°$

Angles in polygons

A **polygon** is a shape made from straight sides.

Any polygon can be divided into triangles by drawing line segments from one vertex to every other vertex. To find the sum of the interior angles, multiply the number of triangles by 180°. There are always two fewer triangles than the number of sides.

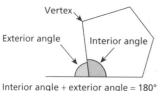

Vertex

Exterior angle   Interior angle

Interior angle + exterior angle = 180°

Pentagon:
5 sides →
3 triangles

Sum of interior angles in a polygon =
(number of sides − 2) × 180°

Sum of exterior angles in a polygon = 360°

A **regular polygon** has sides of equal length and:
- interior angles that are all of equal size
- exterior angles that are all of equal size.

Exterior angle of a regular polygon =
360° ÷ (number of sides)

Interior angle of a regular polygon =
(sum of interior angles) ÷ (number of sides)

a) Work out the size of each exterior angle of a regular pentagon.

A regular pentagon has five sides.

Exterior angle is: $\frac{360°}{5} = 72°$

b) Work out the size of each interior angle of a regular pentagon.

Interior angle + exterior angle = 180°

Interior angle is: $180° - 72° = 108°$

Angle facts and angles in parallel lines

1. Work out the size of the lettered angle in each diagram. Give reasons for your answers.

a)

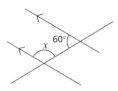

$x = $ _____ °

_____

b)

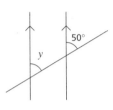

$y = $ _____ °

_____

c)

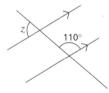

$z = $ _____ °

_____

Angles in polygons

2. The diagram shows a regular pentagon joined to a regular octagon.

Calculate the size of angle x.

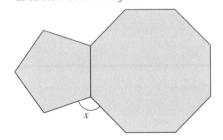

$x = $ _____ °

4 Triangles and quadrilaterals

Triangles

There are four types of triangle.

> The sum of the angles in a triangle is 180°.

Equilateral triangles have three equal sides and three 60° angles.	**Isosceles** triangles have two equal sides and two equal base angles.	**Scalene** triangles have no equal sides and no equal angles.	**Right-angled** triangles have one 90° angle.

Work out the sizes of angle a, b and c.

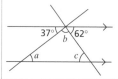

Angle $a = 37°$ ← Angle a is alternate to 37°.

Angle $b = 180° - (37° + 62°) = 81°$ ← Angles on a straight line sum to 180°.

Angle $c = 180° - (37° + 81°) = 62°$ ← Angles in a triangle sum to 180°.

Quadrilaterals

A **quadrilateral** has four sides and four angles.

> The angles in any quadrilateral add up to 360°.

Square

- Four equal sides
- Four 90° angles
- Opposite sides are parallel
- Diagonals bisect each other at right angles

Rectangle

- Two pairs of equal sides
- Four 90° angles
- Opposite sides are parallel
- Diagonals bisect each other

Parallelogram

- Two pairs of equal sides
- Two pairs of equal angles
- Opposite sides are parallel
- Diagonals bisect each other

Rhombus

- Four equal sides
- Two pairs of equal angles
- Opposite sides are parallel
- Diagonals bisect each other at right angles

Kite

- Two pairs of equal sides
- One pair of equal angles
- Diagonals bisect each other at right angles

Trapezium

- One pair of parallel sides

A rhombus is shown. Calculate the values of x and y.

Angle $x = 70°$ ← Opposite angles in a rhombus are equal.

Angle y: $360° - (70° \times 2) = 220°$ ← Angles in a quadrilateral sum to 360°.

$y = 220° \div 2 = 110°$ ← Opposite angles in a rhombus are equal.

Triangles and quadrilaterals

Triangles

1 Calculate the sizes of the lettered angles in each diagram. Give reasons for your answers.

a)

$a =$ _____ °

_____

_____

_____

$b =$ _____ °

_____

_____

_____

b)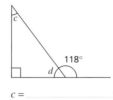

$c =$ _____ °

_____

_____

_____

$d =$ _____ °

_____

_____

_____

c)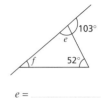

$e =$ _____ °

_____

_____

_____

$f =$ _____ °

_____

_____

_____

Quadrilaterals

2 Write down the name of a quadrilateral with one pair of equal angles. _____

3 a) A kite is shown. Work out the values of a and b. Give reasons for your answers.

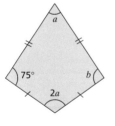

$a =$ _____ °

_____

_____

$b =$ _____ °

_____

_____

b) A trapezium is shown. Work out the sizes of angles c, d and e. Give reasons for your answers.

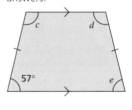

$c =$ _____ °

_____

_____

$d =$ _____ °

_____

_____

$e =$ _____ °

_____

4 Congruence

Congruent shapes

Two or more shapes are **congruent** if they are the same size and the same shape. When a shape is reflected, rotated or translated, the image is congruent to the object.

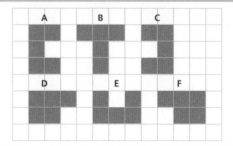

Looking at the shapes shown on the grid:

* shapes A, C and E are congruent to each other
* shapes D and F are congruent to each other.

Congruent triangles

Triangles are congruent if they satisfy any one of the following conditions.

Side, Side, Side (SSS)	Side, Angle, Side (SAS)	Angle, Side, Angle (ASA) or Angle, Angle, Side (AAS)	Right angle, Hypotenuse, Side (RHS)
All three sides of one triangle are equal to the three sides in the other triangle.	Two sides and the included angle of one triangle are equal to the two sides and the included angle in the other triangle.	Both triangles have two equal angles and a corresponding side that is equal in length.	Both triangles have a right angle, an equal hypotenuse and another equal side.
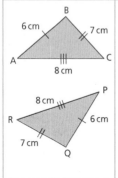	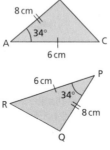	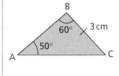 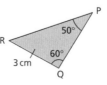	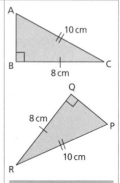
AB = PQ, BC = QR, AC = PR, so congruent (SSS).	AB = PQ, AC = PR, angle A = angle P, so congruent (SAS).	Angle A = angle P, angle B = angle Q, BC = QR, so congruent (AAS).	Angle B = angle Q, AC = PR, BC = QR, so congruent (RHS).

Prove that triangles ABC and PQR are congruent.

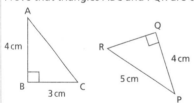

Using Pythagoras' theorem in triangle ABC, AC = 5 cm

Angle B = Angle Q = 90° (right angle)

AC = PR = 5 cm (hypotenuse)

AB = PQ = 4 cm (side)

So the triangles are congruent (RHS).

④ Congruence

Congruent shapes

1. Shapes A to J are shown on the grid.

Complete the sentences.

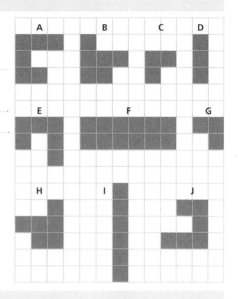

a) Shape A is congruent to shape ....

and shape ....

b) Shape B is congruent to shape ....

c) Shape C is congruent to shape ....

Congruent triangles

2. Decide whether each pair of triangles is congruent or not. Give reasons for your answers.

a)

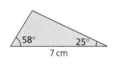

b)

c)

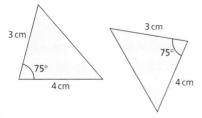

d)

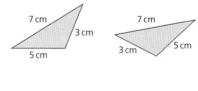

4 Transformations (1)

A transformation may change a shape's position, size or orientation. The original shape is called the **object** and the transformed shape is called the **image**.

Translation

A **translation** moves the original shape.

a) Describe the translation that takes trapezium A to trapezium B.

To describe a translation, state how far the object has moved in each direction, either in words or using vector notation.

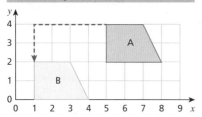

Translation 4 units to the left and 2 down

or translation $\begin{pmatrix} -4 \\ -2 \end{pmatrix}$.

b) Translate trapezium B by the vector $\begin{pmatrix} -1 \\ 2 \end{pmatrix}$. Label the image C.

The vector $\begin{pmatrix} -1 \\ 2 \end{pmatrix}$ is telling you to move 1 unit left and 2 units up.

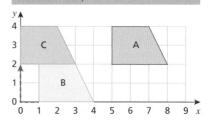

Reflection

A **reflection** transforms a shape so that it's a mirror image of the original shape. The object and the image have line symmetry.

To describe a reflection, give the position or equation of the mirror line, e.g. the x-axis or the line $y = 2$.

Reflect rectangle P in the line $y = x$. Label the image R.

Every point in the image must be the same distance from the line $y = x$ as it is in the object.

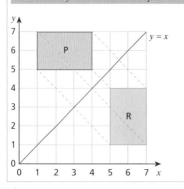

Rotation

A **rotation** transforms a shape so that the original shape is turned about a fixed point. The fixed point is called the **centre of rotation**.

To describe a rotation, state the angle with the direction and the centre of rotation, e.g. a rotation of 90° anticlockwise about (3, 4).

Rotate triangle M 90° clockwise around the point (5, 1). Label the image N.

Trace triangle M, put your pencil on point (5, 1) and turn the tracing paper 90° clockwise. Then draw the image.

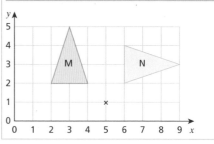

Shapes that have been translated, reflected or rotated are congruent.

Translation

1 Here is an object, A, and its image, B.

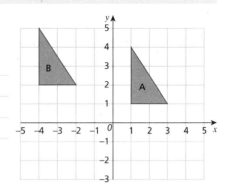

a) Describe the single transformation that takes triangle A onto triangle B.

....

....

....

....

b) Translate triangle B by the vector $\begin{pmatrix} 1 \\ -3 \end{pmatrix}$.
Label the image as triangle C.

Reflection

2 Reflect triangle D in the line $y = x$.
Label the image E.

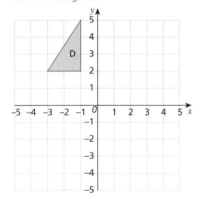

3 Describe the single reflection that takes rectangle P to rectangle Q.

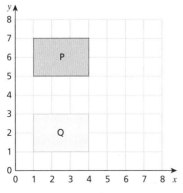

Rotation

4 Rotate triangle F 180° about the origin to form triangle G.

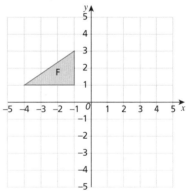

5 Describe the rotation that takes triangle X to triangle Y.

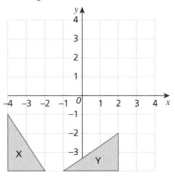

4 Transformations (2)

Enlargement

An enlargement transforms a shape so that the original shape increases or decreases in size.

> A shape that undergone enlargement is **similar** (see page 108) to the object.

The scale factor of an enlargement shows how the lengths of a shape increase or decrease. A scale factor of 2 means that the lengths of each side of a shape double in length. A scale factor of $\frac{1}{2}$ means that the sides halve in length.

Enlargement on a coordinate grid

An enlargement on a coordinate grid takes place from a particular point, the **centre of enlargement**.

Describe the single transformation that takes shape A to shape B.

> To describe an enlargement, state the centre of enlargement and the scale factor of enlargement.

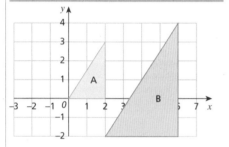

> The lengths have doubled.

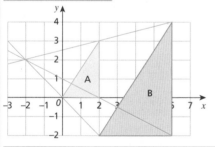

> Draw rays from each vertex in the object to the corresponding vertex in the image. The rays intersect at the centre of enlargement.

Shape B is an enlargement of shape A by a scale factor of 2 from the point (–2, 2).

a) Enlarge rectangle X by a scale factor of 2, centre of enlargement (–2, 2). Label the image Y.

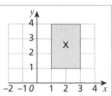

> The first vertex of the object is 2 units up and 3 units to the right from the centre of enlargement. The corresponding vertex of the image is $2 \times 2 = 4$ units up and $3 \times 2 = 6$ units to the right from the centre of enlargement. Repeat for each vertex of the object.

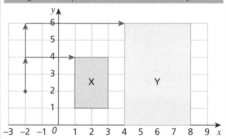

b) Enlarge rectangle X by a scale factor of $\frac{1}{2}$, centre of enlargement (–3, 1). Label the image Z.

> The first vertex of the object is 3 units up and 4 units to the right from the centre of enlargement. The corresponding vertex of the image is $3 \times \frac{1}{2} = 1.5$ units up and $4 \times \frac{1}{2} = 2$ units to the right from the centre of enlargement. Repeat for each vertex of the object.

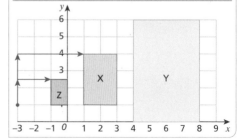

4 Transformations (2)

Enlargement

1 a) Enlarge the trapezium by a scale factor of 3.

b) Enlarge the rectangle by a scale factor of $\frac{1}{2}$.

Enlargement on a coordinate grid

2 Enlarge shape A by a scale factor of 4, centre of enlargement (0, 0).

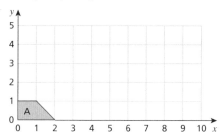

3 Describe the transformation from shape X to shape Y.

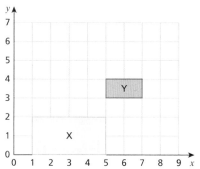

4 3D shapes

Faces, edges and vertices

3D (or **three-dimensional**) shapes are solid figures with three dimensions – length, depth (or width) and height.

Face or **surface:** a flat surface on the shape.

Edge: a line segment where two faces meet.

Vertex (pl. vertices): a corner (where the edges meet).

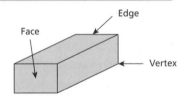

Shape		Faces	Edges	Vertices
Cube	Cuboid	6	12	8
Square-based pyramid		5 1 square and 4 triangles	8	5
Pentagonal prism		7 2 pentagons and 5 rectangles	15	10

The number of faces, edges and vertices in a 3D shape are connected by the formula: $V - E + F = 2$, where V is the number of vertices, E is the number of edges and F is the number of faces.

Cylinders and cones have flat surfaces and curved surfaces. A sphere has a curved surface only.

Cylinder   **Cone**   **Sphere**

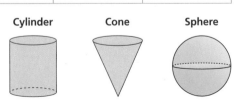

Prisms and pyramids

A prism has a constant **cross-section**. Think of a loaf of bread where each slice is a cross-section. Prisms are named by the shape of their cross-section, e.g. a triangular prism.

A pyramid has a **polygon** as its base and the faces meet at a point.

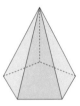

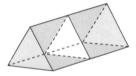

The cross-section of a triangular prism is a triangle, no matter where you slice the shape.

The base of a pentagonal pyramid is a pentagon. The adjoining faces meet at a single point at the top.

3D shapes

Faces, edges and vertices

1 Name each shape shown below.

a)

b)

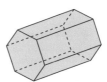

c)

d)

2 Complete the table to show the number of faces, edges and vertices in each shape in question 1.

	Shape	Faces	Edges	Vertices
a)				
b)				
c)				
d)				

Prisms and pyramids

3 Write down the name of the polygon that is the cross-section of each prism.

a)

b)

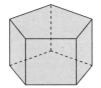

c)

Plans and elevations

Drawing plans and elevations

To draw a plan view, imagine looking at the shape from above. Draw only the parts you would see from above.

Similarly, to draw a side or front elevation, imagine looking at the shape in that direction and draw only what you would see.

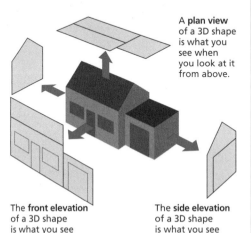

A plan view of a 3D shape is what you see when you look at it from above.

The **front elevation** of a 3D shape is what you see when you look at it from the front.

The **side elevation** of a 3D shape is what you see when you look at it from the side.

Here is a 3D shape made of centimetre cubes drawn on isometric paper:

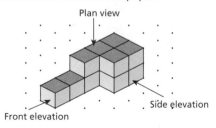

Draw the plan view, the front elevation and the side elevation on squared paper.

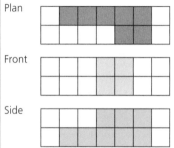

Drawing shapes from plans and elevations

To draw a shape from a plan and elevations, combine the information from all three views to draw the shape on isometric paper.

The three views of a 3D shape are shown below.
Draw the 3D shape on isometric paper.

Plan view   Front elevation

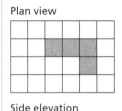

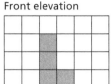

Side elevation

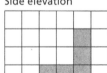

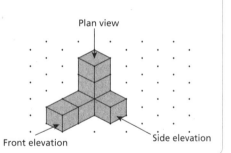

Plans and elevations

Drawing plans and elevations

1. A 3D shape is shown.

   On the grid below, draw the:

   a) plan view

   b) front elevation

   c) side elevation.

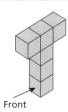

Front

Drawing shapes from plans and elevations

2. Shown below are the plan view, front elevation and side elevation of two 3D shapes.

   Draw each 3D shape on the isometric grids.

a)   Plan view   Front elevation   Side elevation

b)   Plan view   Front elevation   Side elevation

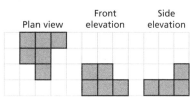

4 Loci and bearings

Locus

The **locus** (plural: **loci**) is the set of points that follows a set of rules or conditions.

You will often need to use constructions to find the locus.

A path is to be laid between two lamp posts, A and B, in a park.

Draw the locus of points that are equidistant from the lamp posts.

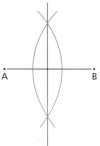

Draw the perpendicular bisector between points A and B.

Bearings

A **bearing** gives the direction to one place from another. Bearings are given using three-figures, e.g. 030° instead of 30°.

To measure a three-figure bearing:
- start from North
- measure clockwise.

If two bearings are in opposite directions, the difference between the bearings is 180°.

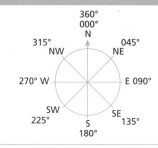

The diagram shows a map drawn to scale showing two towns, A and B.

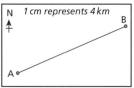

1 cm represents 4 km

a) Write the bearing from A to B.

Line the protractor up so that it is facing North and measure the angle clockwise. The angle is 67°.

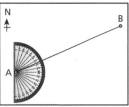

The bearing from A to B is 067°.

b) Work out the actual distance from A to B.

The real distance is 3.2 × 4 = 12.8 km

Multiply the actual distance by 4 as the scale is given as 1 cm represents 4 km.

c) Work out the bearing of A from B.

The bearing from B to A is 247°.

Given the bearing from A to B is 067°, the bearing from B to A is 180° + 067° = 247°.

4 Loci and bearings

Locus

1. A mobile phone is plugged into a wall charger of length 3 m.

Show the locus of points that the phone will reach while plugged in for charging.
Use a scale of 1 cm = 1 m.

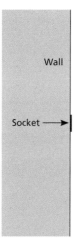

Wall

Socket ➔|

Bearings

2. Here is a map of four towns, A, B, C and D.

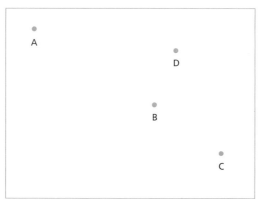

Work out the bearing of:

a) A from B .... °

b) C from B .... °

c) D from B .... °

4 Perimeter and area

Perimeter

The perimeter of a shape is the total distance around the outside edge.

A compound shape is made up from other shapes such as squares, rectangles and triangles.

When working out the perimeter of a compound shape, remember to only count the outside edges (not any edges inside the shape).

Two shapes, A and B, are shown on a centimetre square grid. Which has the greater perimeter?

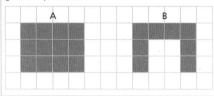

It may help to number along the edges of the diagrams. It's not enough to just work out the perimeters. You have to state which is greater.

Perimeter of shape A is:
$4 + 3 + 4 + 3 = 14$ cm

Perimeter of shape B is:
$3 + 1 + 2 + 2 + 2 + 1 + 3 + 4 = 18$ cm

So shape B has the greater perimeter.

Area

You need to know how to find the area of a triangle, trapezium and parallelogram, and how to use them to find the area of a compound shape.

To find the area of a compound shape, break it down into its simpler component shapes and add their areas together.

Area of triangle $= \frac{1}{2} \times$ base $\times$ perpendicular height

$A = \frac{1}{2}bh$

Perpendicular height, h

Base, b

Area of trapezium $= \frac{1}{2}(a + b)h$

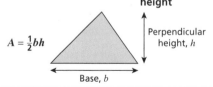

Area of a parallelogram $=$ base $\times$ perpendicular height

$A = bh$

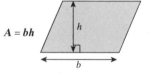

Work out the area of each shape.

a)

5.4 cm

6.2 cm

Area of triangle $= \frac{1}{2} \times 6.2 \times 5.4$
$= 16.74$ cm²

b)

3.5 cm

4 cm

7.5 cm

Area of trapezium $= \frac{1}{2} \times (3.5 + 7.5) \times 4$
$= 22$ cm²

c)

6 cm   7 cm

8 cm

Don't mix up the perpendicular height with the sloping height.

Area of a parallelogram $= 8 \times 6$
$= 48$ cm²

4 Perimeter and area

Perimeter

1 Work out the perimeter of each shape.

a)

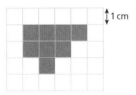

$\updownarrow$ 1 cm

b)

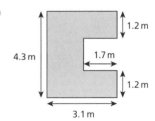

1.2 m

4.3 m

1.7 m

1.2 m

3.1 m

Perimeter = _____ cm

Perimeter = _____ m

Area

2 Work out the area of each shape.

a)

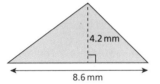

4.2 mm

8.6 mm

b)

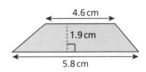

4.6 cm

1.9 cm

5.8 cm

Area = _____ mm²

Area = _____ cm²

c)

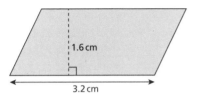

1.6 cm

3.2 cm

d)

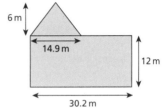

6 m

14.9 m

12 m

30.2 m

Area = _____ cm²

Area = _____ m²

(4) Circles

Circle facts

- The **circumference** of a circle is the distance around the edge of the circle (its perimeter).
- The **radius** of a circle is a straight line from the centre to the circumference.
- The **diameter** is a straight line through the centre joining opposite points on the circumference.
- A **chord** is a straight line joining any two points on the circumference.

- A **tangent** is a straight line that touches the circumference of a circle.
- An **arc** is a part of the circumference of a circle.
- A **sector** is the area enclosed by two radii and an arc.
- A **segment** is the area between a chord and its arc.

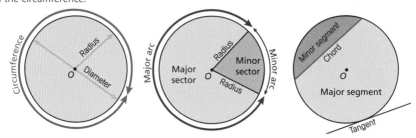

Circumference and area of circles

Circumference = π × diameter or $C = \pi d$

Circumference = 2 × π × radius or $C = 2\pi r$

Area = π × radius²

$$A = \pi r^2$$

a) Calculate the circumference of this circle to 2 decimal places.

5.4 cm

$C = 2\pi r$

$= 2 \times \pi \times 5.4$

$= 33.929...$

$= 33.93$ cm

You could get the same answer by working out the diameter (2 × 5.4 = 10.8 cm), then using the formula $C = \pi d$.

b) Work out the area of the circle to 2 decimal places.

$A = \pi r^2 = \pi \times 5.4 \times 5.4$

$= 91.608...$

$= 91.61$ cm²

Sector area and arc length

A **sector** is a fraction of a circle, so the sector area is a fraction of the area.

An **arc** is a fraction of the perimeter of the circle, so the arc length is a fraction of the circumference.

Area of sector = $\frac{\text{angle at centre}}{360°}$ × area of circle

Arc length = $\frac{\text{angle at centre}}{360°}$ × circumference of circle

Work out the arc length and the area of the sector to 1 decimal place.

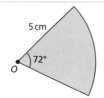

5 cm

72°

O

Arc length = $\frac{\text{angle at centre}}{360°}$ × circumference of circle

$= \frac{72°}{360°} \times 2 \times \pi \times 5 = 6.3$ cm

Area of sector = $\frac{\text{angle at centre}}{360°}$ × area of circle

$= \frac{72°}{360°} \times \pi \times 5^2 = 15.7$ cm²

Circles

Circle facts

1 Label the parts of the circle shown.

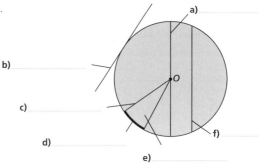

a) ....

b) ....

c) ....

d) ....

e) ....

f) ....

Circumference and area of circles

2 Work out the circumference and area of each circle, giving your answers to 1 decimal place.

a)

O•---------- 3.2 cm

Circumference = ... cm

Area = ... cm²

b)

O
5.8 m

Circumference = ... m

Area = ... m²

Sector area and arc length

3 A sector is shown.

Work out the following, giving your answers to 2 decimal places.

120°

O   5 cm

a) The arc length of the sector

.... cm

b) The area of the sector

.... cm²

Surface area and volume

Surface area

The **surface area** of a 3D shape is the total area of all the surfaces (faces) added together. For example, the surface area of a cube is the total area of the six squares of its net.

> The surface area is equal to the area of the net of the shape.

Work out the surface area of this shape.

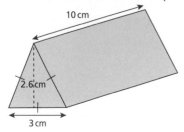

> The net of a triangular prism shows that it has two triangular faces and three rectangular faces.

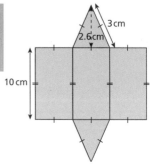

> Add up the area of all the faces.

Area of each triangle is $\frac{1}{2} \times 3 \times 2.6 = 3.9\,\text{cm}^2$

Area of each rectangle is $3 \times 10 = 30\,\text{cm}^2$

Total surface area is $3.9 + 3.9 + 30 + 30 + 30 = 97.8\,\text{cm}^2$

Volume of prisms

The **volume** of a prism is always the product of the area of the cross-section and the length (or depth) of the prism. The units for volume are cubed, e.g. cm³ or m³.

Cylinders are special types of prisms. The cross-section of a cylinder is a circle.

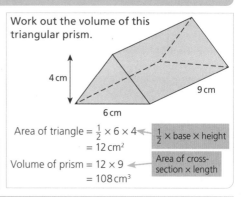

Volume of a cuboid = length × width × height
Volume of a prism = area of cross-section × length
Volume of a cylinder = π × radius² × height

Work out the volume of this triangular prism.

Area of triangle $= \frac{1}{2} \times 6 \times 4$ ← $\frac{1}{2} \times$ base × height
$= 12\,\text{cm}^2$

Volume of prism $= 12 \times 9$ ← Area of cross-section × length
$= 108\,\text{cm}^3$

Volume of spheres, pyramids and cones

You should also know how to use the formulae for finding the volume of spheres, pyramids and cones.

Volume of a sphere $= \frac{4}{3}\pi r^3$
Volume of a pyramid $= \frac{1}{3} \times$ area of base × vertical height
Volume of a cone $= \frac{1}{3} \times \pi r^2 h$

Work out the volume of this cone.

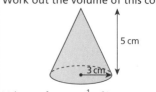

Volume of cone $= \frac{1}{3}\pi r^2 h$
Volume $= \frac{1}{3} \times \pi \times 3 \times 3 \times 5$
$= 15\pi\,\text{cm}^3$ or $47.1\,\text{cm}^3$

Surface area and volume

Surface area

1. Work out the surface area of each shape.

a)

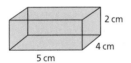

2 cm

4 cm

5 cm

Surface area = _____ cm²

b)

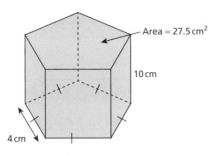

Area = 27.5 cm²

10 cm

4 cm

Surface area = _____ cm²

Volume of prisms

2. Work out the volume of each shape in question 1.

a)

Volume = _____ cm³

b)

Volume = _____ cm³

Volume of spheres, pyramids and cones

3. Calculate the volume of the sphere.

Volume of a sphere = $\frac{4}{3}\pi r^3$

6 m

Volume = _____ m³

4. Work out the volume of the pyramid.

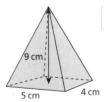

Volume of a pyramid = $\frac{1}{3}$ × area of base × vertical height

9 cm

5 cm

4 cm

Volume = _____ cm³

Similar figures and scale drawings

Similar shapes and working out lengths

Two shapes are **similar** if one shape is an enlargement of the other:
- The angles in one shape will be equal to the corresponding angles in the other shape.
- The corresponding sides of each shape are in the same ratio.

Show that triangle ACE is similar to triangle BCD.

Sketching the two separate triangles will help you to visualise them.

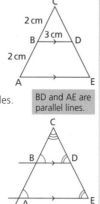

Angle A = Angle B because they are corresponding angles.

Similarly, angle D = angle E.

Angle C is in both triangles.

All the corresponding angles are equal, so triangle ACE is similar to triangle BCD.

BD and AE are parallel lines.

Are these two triangles similar? Give reasons for your answer.

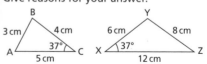

Angle X corresponds to angle C so side AB corresponds to side YZ.

Side AC corresponds to XZ and side BC corresponds to XY.

AB = 3 cm and YZ = 8 cm. 8 ÷ 3 = 2.6̇

XY = 6 cm and BC = 4 cm. 6 ÷ 4 = 1.5

The sides are not in the same ratio, so the triangles are **not** similar.

To work out a missing length:
1. Find the scale factor by dividing two corresponding lengths.
2. Multiply the known corresponding length by the scale factor.

Triangles ABC and PQR are similar. Work out the length of PR.

AB corresponds to PQ, so to find the scale factor divide PQ by AB.

7.5 ÷ 5 = 1.5

AC corresponds to PR, so the length of PR is 8 × 1.5 = 12 cm

Scale drawings

A scale drawing is a representation of a shape or distance with accurate lengths reduced by a given **scale factor**. Scale factors can be given in words or as ratios, e.g. 1 cm represents 5 km or 1 : 500 000.

Use the map to work out the actual distance between London and Birmingham.

Measure the distance from London to Birmingham on the map: it is 2.8 cm.

2.8 × 60 = 168 km

The scale is 1 cm represents 60 km, so multiply the distance by 60 to find the distance in kilometres.

Scale: 1 cm represents 60 km

• Birmingham

London •

4 Similar figures and scale drawings

Similar shapes and working out lengths

1 Show that these two triangles are similar.

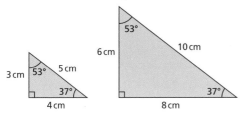

....

....

....

2 Work out the length of CE in the diagram below.

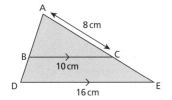

CE = ... cm

Scale drawings

3 Look at the map below.

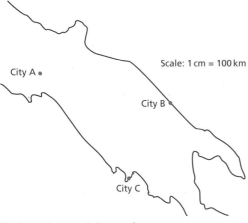

Scale: 1 cm = 100 km

City A •

City B •

City C

Work out the actual distance from:

a) City A to City B .... km

b) City B to City C .... km

(4) Pythagoras' theorem

Pythagoras in right-angled triangles

A **right-angled triangle** is a triangle that contains a right angle. The side opposite the right angle is called the **hypotenuse**, and is usually written as either h or c.

 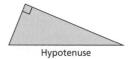

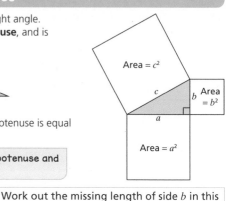

Pythagoras' theorem states that the square on the hypotenuse is equal to the sum of the squares on the other two sides.

> Pythagoras theorem is $a^2 + b^2 = c^2$ where c is the hypotenuse and a and b are the other two sides.

Work out the length of the hypotenuse in this right-angled triangle.

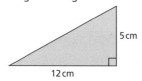

Pythagoras' theorem states that $c^2 = a^2 + b^2$

So c^2 is $12^2 + 5^2 = 144 + 25$

$c^2 = 169$

So c is $\sqrt{169} = 13\,\text{cm}$

Work out the missing length of side b in this right-angled triangle.

Pythagoras' theorem states that $a^2 + b^2 = c^2$

$21^2 + b^2 = 29^2$

$b^2 = 29^2 - 21^2$

$b = \sqrt{29^2 - 21^2} = 20\,\text{cm}$

Make sure you substitute the values for the correct variable.

Using Pythagoras' theorem to solve problems

You will often need to use Pythagoras' theorem in order to solve other problems.

Work out the area of this isosceles triangle.

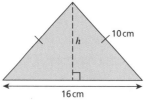

$10^2 = h^2 + 8^2$

$100 = h^2 + 64$

$100 - 64 = h^2$

$36 = h^2$

So $h = 6\,\text{cm}$

Area $= \frac{1}{2} \times 16 \times 6 \longleftarrow \frac{1}{2} \times \text{base} \times \text{height}$

Area $= 48\,\text{cm}^2$

An isosceles triangle can be broken up into two right-angled triangles, so you can use Pythagoras' theorem to work out the height. You then have all the information you need to work out the area.

4 Pythagoras' theorem

Pythagoras in right-angled triangles

1 Work out the missing side length in each triangle.

a) Give your answer to 2 decimal places.

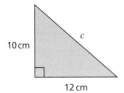

10 cm

c

12 cm

c = _____ cm

b)

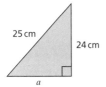

25 cm

24 cm

a

a = _____ cm

Using Pythagoras' theorem to solve problems

2 Work out the area of this triangle.

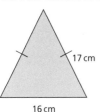

17 cm

16 cm

_____ cm²

3 Work out the area of this rectangle.

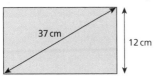

37 cm

12 cm

_____ cm²

4 Trigonometry

Using the trigonometric ratios to work out sides and angles

Trigonometry is used to work out unknown lengths or unknown angles in **right-angled triangles**.

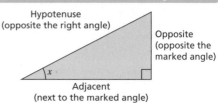

Hypotenuse
(opposite the right angle)

Opposite
(opposite the marked angle)

Adjacent
(next to the marked angle)

> The three trigonometrical ratios you need to know are called **sine, cosine** and **tangent**. Remember SOH CAH TOA.

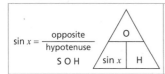

$$\sin x = \frac{\text{opposite}}{\text{hypotenuse}}$$

SOH

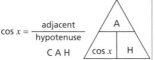

$$\cos x = \frac{\text{adjacent}}{\text{hypotenuse}}$$

CAH

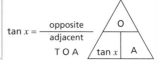

$$\tan x = \frac{\text{opposite}}{\text{adjacent}}$$

TOA

To work out a length using trigonometry:
1. Label the sides (hyp, opp, adj) in this order.
2. Identify the given side and the one to find.
3. Choose the correct ratio.
4. Set up and solve the equation.

To work out an angle using trigonometry:
1. Label the sides (hyp, opp, adj) in this order.
2. Identify the two given sides.
3. Choose the correct ratio.
4. Set up and solve the equation.

Work out the length x.

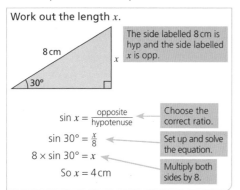

8 cm

x

30°

The side labelled 8 cm is hyp and the side labelled x is opp.

$$\sin x = \frac{\text{opposite}}{\text{hypotenuse}}$$ Choose the correct ratio.

$$\sin 30° = \frac{x}{8}$$ Set up and solve the equation.

$$8 \times \sin 30° = x$$ Multiply both sides by 8.

So $x = 4$ cm

Work out the size of angle x.

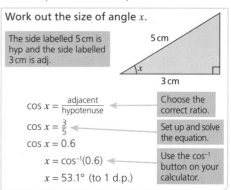

5 cm

x

3 cm

The side labelled 5 cm is hyp and the side labelled 3 cm is adj.

$$\cos x = \frac{\text{adjacent}}{\text{hypotenuse}}$$ Choose the correct ratio.

$$\cos x = \frac{3}{5}$$ Set up and solve the equation.

$$\cos x = 0.6$$

$$x = \cos^{-1}(0.6)$$ Use the $\cos^{-1}$ button on your calculator.

$$x = 53.1° \text{ (to 1 d.p.)}$$

> To find a missing angle, ensure you can use inverse trigonometric ratios on your calculator.

Solving real-life problems using trigonometry

An **angle of elevation** is the angle measured above a horizontal direction.

An **angle of depression** is the angle measured below a horizontal direction.

A builder stands 5 metres from a building. He is 1.8 metres tall.

Work out the building's height.

> Work out the height in the same way that you would find an unknown length in any right-angled triangle but remember to add on the height of the builder.

40°

5 m

1.8 m

$$\tan x = \frac{\text{opposite}}{\text{adjacent}}$$ Use x for the height of the triangle.

$$\tan 40° = \frac{x}{5}$$

$$5 \times \tan 40° = x$$ Multiply both sides by 5.

$$x = 4.2 \text{ m (to 1 d.p.)}$$

So height of building is $4.2 + 1.8 = 6$ metres

Using the trigonometric ratios to work out sides and angles

1 Work out the value of x in each diagram. Give your answers to 2 decimal places where appropriate.

a)

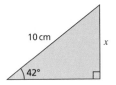

10 cm

x

42°

$x =$ .... cm

b)

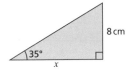

8 cm

35°

x

$x =$ .... cm

c)

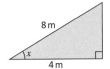

8 m

x

4 m

$x =$ .... °

Solving real-life problems using trigonometry

2 A surveyor stands 20 m from a building and measures the angle of elevation to the top of the building to be 60°.

Calculate the height of the building to the nearest metre.

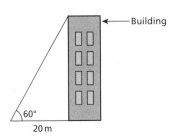

Building

60°

20 m

.... m

Introduction to vectors

A **vector** is line segment of a certain length (magnitude) and a particular direction.

A **scalar** is a number with magnitude only and no direction.

A vector can be written using an arrow to show its direction between two points, e.g. $\overrightarrow{AB}$, or it can be written with a bold, lowercase letter, e.g. **a**. When writing a vector by hand, underline the letter, e.g. a.

A vector can be represented in **column notation**, which tells you the magnitude in each direction,

$$\begin{pmatrix} \text{change in } x \\ \text{change in } y \end{pmatrix}.$$

> Vectors are equal if they have the same length and direction, no matter where they are on a grid. A negative vector has the same magnitude but the opposite direction.

Draw vectors $\overrightarrow{AB} = \begin{pmatrix} 3 \\ -4 \end{pmatrix}$ and $\overrightarrow{CD} = \begin{pmatrix} 3 \\ -4 \end{pmatrix}$ on a grid.

Both vectors go 3 units in the x direction and -4 units in the y direction.

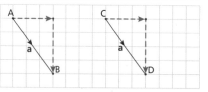

The vectors are equal – they have the same magnitude and the same direction, even though they start at different points.

Given vector **u**, draw vector −**u**.

Vectors **u** and −**u** will have the same magnitude but they will point in opposite directions.

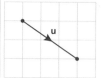 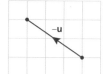

Calculating with vectors

Adding and subtracting vectors:

1. Draw the vectors 'nose to tail' so that they join up.
2. Add each component to find the resultant vector, **a** + **b**.
3. To subtract a vector on a diagram, reverse the direction.

> When adding vectors, $\overrightarrow{AB} + \overrightarrow{BC} = \overrightarrow{AC}$

A vector that has been **multiplied by a scalar** (a number) is a multiple of that vector in the same direction.

Here, vector $\overrightarrow{CD} = 2 \times \overrightarrow{AB}$.

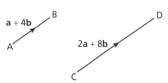

$\mathbf{a} = \begin{pmatrix} 4 \\ 3 \end{pmatrix}$ and $\mathbf{b} = \begin{pmatrix} 3 \\ -1 \end{pmatrix}$

a) Work out **a** + **b**.

$$\mathbf{a} + \mathbf{b} = \begin{pmatrix} 4 \\ 3 \end{pmatrix} + \begin{pmatrix} 3 \\ -1 \end{pmatrix} = \begin{pmatrix} 4+3 \\ 3-1 \end{pmatrix} = \begin{pmatrix} 7 \\ 2 \end{pmatrix}$$

b) Work out **a** − **b**.

$$\mathbf{a} - \mathbf{b} = \begin{pmatrix} 4 \\ 3 \end{pmatrix} - \begin{pmatrix} 3 \\ -1 \end{pmatrix} = \begin{pmatrix} 4-3 \\ 3+1 \end{pmatrix} = \begin{pmatrix} 1 \\ 4 \end{pmatrix}$$

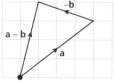

Vectors

Introduction to vectors

1 A is the point (1, 2). $\overrightarrow{AB} = \begin{pmatrix} 5 \\ -3 \end{pmatrix}$.

Work out the coordinates of B.

Calculating with vectors

2 ABCD is a trapezium of three equilateral triangles.

$\overrightarrow{OA} = \mathbf{a}$ and $\overrightarrow{DC} = \mathbf{b}$

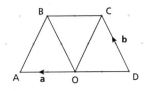

Express the following vectors in terms of **a** and **b**.

a) $\overrightarrow{BC}$

b) $\overrightarrow{BD}$

c) $\overrightarrow{CO}$

3 $\overrightarrow{OA} = \mathbf{a}$

$\overrightarrow{OB} = \mathbf{b}$

$\overrightarrow{OC} = 2\mathbf{a} - 3\mathbf{b}$

Work out the following vectors.

a) $\overrightarrow{BA}$

b) $\overrightarrow{AC}$

5 Theoretical probability

Probability

Probability is the chance or likelihood of something happening on a scale of 0 to 1.

> Probabilities can be written as fractions, decimals or percentages.

An **event** is anything that is used to measure the probability of something, e.g. rolling a dice.

An **outcome** is the result of an event, e.g. rolling a 2.

Equally likely outcomes each have the same probability of happening, e.g. rolling a 3 or rolling a 4 on a fair, 1-to-6 dice both have a probability of $\frac{1}{6}$

> The probability of an outcome, A, occurring is written as P(A).

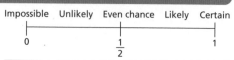

Describe in words the probability of:

a) next month having 32 days.

Impossible ← No month has 32 days.

b) being the winner of a lottery.

Unlikely ← You are not likely to be the winner.

c) getting heads or tails on a coin flip.

Certain ← The only possible outcomes are heads or tails.

Probability of an outcome

Theoretical probability is calculated by considering the number of ways an outcome can occur. This contrasts with experimental probability (see page 118).

The theoretical probability of an outcome can be found using the formula:

$$P(\text{outcome}) = \frac{\text{number of ways the outcome can happen}}{\text{total number of possible outcomes}}$$

Write the probability of rolling an even number on a fair dice numbered 1 to 6.

Three out of the six numbers are even: 2, 4, and 6.

$P(\text{even}) = \frac{3}{6}$ (or $\frac{1}{2}$ or 50%)

In a class, 12 students brought a packed lunch and 16 had school dinners.

What is the probability that a student chosen at random brought a packed lunch?

$P(\text{packed lunch}) = \frac{12}{28}$ or $\frac{3}{7}$ | 12 out of 28 students brought a packed lunch.

Mutually exclusive events

Mutually exclusive events cannot happen at the same time.

The probabilities of mutually exclusive events add to 1.

For example, the probability of rolling a 2 on a fair, six-sided dice is $\frac{1}{6}$ so the probability of not rolling a 2 is $1 - \frac{1}{6} = \frac{5}{6}$

> If events are mutually exclusive, the probability of an outcome p **not** happening is $1 - p$.

In a drawer there are only blue and black socks.

The probability of picking a black sock at random is $\frac{3}{5}$.

a) What is the probability of picking a blue sock?

P(blue) is $1 - P(\text{black}) = 1 - \frac{3}{5} = \frac{2}{5}$

b) There are 4 more black socks than blue socks. How many socks are in the drawer?

Start by working out what fraction 4 socks is of all the socks in the drawer. You can then use this fraction to work out the total number of socks.

The probability of picking a black sock is $\frac{1}{5}$ greater than picking a blue sock.

So the extra 4 socks must represent $\frac{3}{5} - \frac{2}{5} = \frac{1}{5}$ of the total socks in the drawer.

$4 \times 5 = 20$ socks in total ← 12 black and 8 blue

5 Theoretical probability

Probability

1 Choose the best option from the box to describe the probability of each event below.

| impossible | unlikely | even chance | likely | certain |

a) Rolling a 7 on a dice numbered 1 to 6 ....

b) Drawing a red card from a pack that is half red and half black ....

c) Next week having 7 days ....

d) Taking a red ball from a bag containing 10 red balls and 90 green balls ....

Probability of an outcome

2 Here is a spinner:

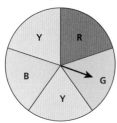

Write down the probability that the spinner lands on yellow. ....

3 The letters of the word MATHEMATICS are placed in a hat.

Calculate the probability of randomly choosing the letter M.

Mutually exclusive events

4 A weather forecast says the probability of rain tomorrow is 81%.

Write down the probability that it will **not** rain tomorrow.

5 Look at the spinner in question 2.

Write the probability that the spinner does **not** land on yellow.

5 Experimental probability

Relative frequency

Experimental probability is useful when it is not possible to find a theoretical probability (see page 116), such as when predicting the weather. Trials are performed and results are recorded to find an **estimated probability** or **relative frequency.**

Experimental probability can also be used to determine **fairness** or **bias**.

An experiment is a set of trials or samples of a population.

> The experimental probability will get closer to the theoretical probability as an unbiased experiment is performed more times or the sample size is increased.

For example, take the case of rolling a dice:
- The experiment is the dice roll.
- The sample space is the set of all possible outcomes, e.g. the numbers 1 to 6.
- An outcome is the result of the experiment, e.g. rolling a 3.
- An event is the set of outcomes, e.g. in the event of rolling an even number, the set of outcomes is 2, 4 and 6.

A trial or experiment is fair or unbiased when each outcome is equally likely. It is biased when the outcomes are not equally likely.

The relative frequency of an event is an estimated probability, based on the outcomes of an experiment.

$$\text{Relative frequency} = \frac{\text{number of times outcome occurs}}{\text{total number of trials}}$$

Shannon suspects that a dice is biased towards landing on 3.

a) Calculate the theoretical probability of the dice landing on 3.

> When comparing probabilities, it is often easiest to convert them to decimals or percentages.

$P(3) = \frac{1}{6} = 0.1\dot{6}$

b) Shannon rolls the dice 100 times. The table shows the results. Calculate the relative frequency of the dice landing on 3.

Number	1	2	3	4	5	6
Frequency	14	15	22	18	15	16

Relative frequency $= \frac{22}{100} = 0.22$ It landed on '3' 22 times out of 100.

c) Shannon rolls the dice another 100 times and lands on 3 on 12 occasions. Calculate the new relative frequency.

Relative frequency $= \frac{34}{200} = 0.17$

> $\frac{34}{200}$ is a better estimate than $\frac{22}{100}$ because it is based on more trials.

d) Is Shannon correct to think that the dice is biased?

The dice does not appear to be biased as the relative frequency after 200 trials is close to the theoretical probability.

Expected outcomes

Another way to compare theoretical and experimental results is by calculating the number of times you expect an outcome to occur. This is called the **expected frequency**.

Expected frequency = number of trials × probability of the event

---

Estimate the number of times you would expect the spinner to land on red if it were spun:

a) 5 times

$P(\text{red}) = \frac{2}{8} = \frac{1}{4}$

Expected frequency $= 5 \times \frac{1}{4} = 1.25$

> The expected frequency does not have to be an integer.

b) 20 times

Expected frequency $= 20 \times \frac{1}{4} = 5$

c) Mo spins the spinner 20 times and gets red 8 times. He decides the spinner is biased. Do you agree?

Although 8 is greater than 5, he should spin the spinner more times to decide if it is biased. 20 is not a very large sample size.

Experimental probability

Relative frequency

1 Belle spins this spinner and records the results in a table.

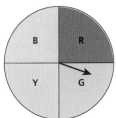

Colour	Blue	Red	Green	Yellow
Frequency	15	20	18	7
Relative frequency				

a) Complete the table. Give the relative frequencies to 2 decimal places.

b) Belle suspects the spinner is biased.

Do you agree? Give a reason for your answer.

....

....

....

Expected outcomes

2 Amira's class counts butterflies in their gardens over a one-week period. The table shows the results.

Species	Red admiral	Gatekeeper	Large white	Small white	Meadow brown
Frequency	26	19	22	18	15

a) Calculate the relative frequency of red admiral butterflies.

....

b) If there are 700 butterflies in Amira's local park, estimate how many of them will be red admirals.

....

Sample spaces and combined events

Sample spaces

The **sample space** is the set of all possible outcomes of an event, e.g. rolling a 1, 2, 3, 4, 5 or 6 on a six-sided dice. The notation S = { } is often used to show the sample space.

Sample spaces of combined events can be shown in various ways, such as in a list or as a table.

The sample space of a six-sided dice is S = {1, 2, 3, 4, 5, 6}

a) A spinner is spun and a coin is flipped. Show the sample space of the outcomes.

There are two possible outcomes for the coin and four possible outcomes for the spinner so there are 4 × 2 = 8 possible outcomes.

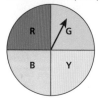

		Spinner			
		Red	**Green**	**Yellow**	**Blue**
Coin	**Heads**	H, R	H, G	H, Y	H, B
	Tails	T, R	T, G	T, Y	T, B

b) Work out the probability of obtaining a sum of 10 when rolling two dice.

		Dice 1					
		1	**2**	**3**	**4**	**5**	**6**
Dice 2	**1**	2	3	4	5	6	7
	2	3	4	5	6	7	8
	3	4	5	6	7	8	9
	4	5	6	7	8	9	⑩
	5	6	7	8	9	⑩	11
	6	7	8	9	⑩	11	12

To find all the possible outcomes, make a table showing the outcome of the first dice, the second dice and their sum.

There are three ways to roll a sum of 10.

P(sum of 10) = $\frac{3}{36}$ or $\frac{1}{12}$

There are 6 × 6 = 36 possible outcomes.

Probability of combined events

More than one event may occur to give an outcome, e.g. a dice roll and a coin flip. To find the probability of two or more **combined events**, e.g. P(6 and heads), record the sample space and use the probability formula:

P(outcome) = $\frac{\text{number of ways the outcome can happen}}{\text{total number of possible outcomes}}$

Two events are **independent** if the outcome of one event does not affect the outcome of the other, e.g. a dice roll does not affect a coin flip.

The product rule of independent events is
P(A and B) = P(A) × P(B)

A coin is flipped and a fair, six-sided dice numbered 1 to 6 is rolled. Work out the probability of getting tails and an odd number.

		Dice					
		1	**2**	**3**	**4**	**5**	**6**
Coin	**Heads**	H, 1	H, 2	H, 3	H, 4	H, 5	H, 6
	Tails	T, 1	T, 2	T, 3	T, 4	T, 5	T, 6

There are three possible outcomes for tails and an odd number.

P(tails and odd) = $\frac{3}{12} = \frac{1}{4}$

There are 12 outcomes in total.

Alternatively, using the product rule for independent events, P(tails and odd) = P(tails) × P(odd) = $\frac{1}{2} \times \frac{1}{2} = \frac{1}{4}$

5 Sample spaces and combined events

Sample spaces

1 A game is played by rolling two fair, six-sided dice and working out their product.

Complete the sample space diagram showing the possible outcomes.

	Dice 1					

(Dice 2 label on left axis)

2 These two spinners are spun.

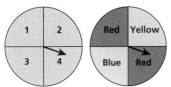

Draw a sample space diagram
showing the possible outcomes.

Probability of combined events

3 Use your answer to question 2 to calculate the probability of landing on red and rolling a 4.

4 Use the product rule of independent events to confirm your answer to question 3.

⑤ Tree diagrams

Frequency trees

A **frequency tree** shows the frequency of the outcomes (or sample space) of two events. Branches show the outcomes of each event.

> The probability of each outcome is the experimental probability, or relative frequency.

To draw a frequency tree:
1. Start with a single point. Draw branches for each possible outcome.
2. Write the outcomes at the end of each branch.
3. Write the frequency on each branch.
4. Repeat for each event, starting with the outcome of the previous event.

In a school, there are 10 maths teachers and 12 science teachers.
7 of the maths teachers like tea. 5 of the science teachers do not like tea.

a) Draw a frequency tree to represent the sample space.

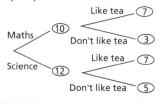

b) How many maths and science teachers do not like tea in total?
3 maths teachers and 5 science teachers don't like tea, so 8 teachers do not like tea.

c) Calculate the probability that a person chosen at random from the maths and science teachers does not like tea.
8 teachers out of 22 do not like tea, so
P(teacher does not like tea) = $\frac{8}{22}$ or $\frac{4}{11}$

Tree diagrams

A tree diagram is similar to a frequency tree; however, it shows the probability of each event rather than the frequency. It is especially useful for calculating probabilities of dependent events.

> To find the probability of combined events, multiply the probability of the outcomes along each branch.

To draw a tree diagram:
1. Start with a single point. Draw branches corresponding to the possible outcomes.
2. Write the outcomes of the first event at the end of each branch.
3. Work out the probability of each outcome and write it on each branch. The probabilities of each set of branches should sum to 1.
4. Repeat for each event, starting with the outcome of the previous event.

At a school, students have either a school dinner or bring packed lunch. The probability of a student ordering a school dinner is 0.3. Two students are chosen at random.

a) Use a tree diagram to work out the probability of both students ordering school dinners.

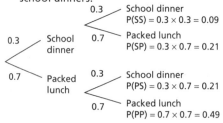

P(SS) = P(1st school dinner) × P(2nd school dinner) = 0.3 × 0.3 = 0.09 | P(A and B) = P(A) × P(B)

b) Use the tree diagram to work out the probability of exactly one of the students ordering school dinners.

> There are two ways this outcome can occur. The first student could order school dinner and the second student have packed lunch, or vice-versa.

P(exactly one school dinner) = P(PS) + P(SP)
= 0.21 + 0.21
= 0.42

⑤ Tree diagrams

Frequency trees

1 A yoga and Pilates studio has 180 members.
80 members attend classes in the morning and the remaining members attend classes in the evening.
Of the members who attend in the morning, 30 prefer yoga and the rest prefer Pilates.
Of the evening members, 40 prefer Pilates and the rest prefer yoga.

a) Draw a frequency tree to show this information.

b) Calculate the probability that a member chosen at random prefers Pilates classes.

Tree diagrams

2 A bag contains 7 yellow and 3 blue marbles. A marble is picked at random, replaced in the bag, and another marble is then picked at random.

a) Draw a tree diagram to represent the probabilities of picking each colour of marble.

b) Work out the probability of picking two yellow marbles.

5 Venn diagrams

Interpreting Venn diagrams

A **set** is a collection of things. It could be the set of all even numbers, the set of factors of 30, or the set of workers who are part-time.

A **Venn diagram** shows the relationship between two or more **sets** and is a visual representation of what they do and do not have in common.

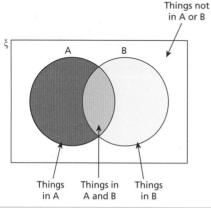

Things not in A or B

Things in A

Things in A and B

Things in B

You can use a Venn diagram to calculate probabilities.

This Venn diagram shows which shifts some members of staff work at a company.

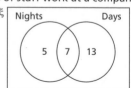

ξ Nights   Days
    5 7 13

a) How many members of staff work night shifts?

5 + 7 = 12 staff work night shifts

Add the numbers in the 'Nights' circle: the 5 who work nights only and the 7 in the intersection who work both nights and days.

b) How many members of staff does the company have in total?

The company has a total of 5 + 7 + 13 = 25 staff

Add up all the numbers in the Venn diagram.

c) What is the probability that a member of staff chosen at random works both night and day shifts?

P(both shifts) = $\frac{7}{25}$

7 out of 25 workers work both shifts.

Drawing Venn diagrams

To draw a Venn diagram:

1. Draw overlapping circles representing each set and label them.
2. Fill in any sections that can be completed without calculation from the information given.
3. Work out the outstanding sections (e.g. a value in the intersection may enable you to find a missing value for one of the circles).
4. Check your final diagram against any totals given in the question.

There are 28 students in a class:

- 12 students study Spanish.
- 15 students study French.
- 3 students study both French and Spanish.
- The rest do not study either language.

a) Draw a Venn diagram to show this information.

b) Use the Venn diagram to work out the probability that a randomly chosen student studies only French.

12 students out of 28 study only French.

So P(only French) = $\frac{12}{28}$ or $\frac{3}{7}$

3 students study both French and Spanish.

ξ S   F
   9 3 12
          4

Of the 15 students that study French, 3 study both French and Spanish, so there are 15 − 3 = 12 students who study only French.

12 + 15 − 3 = 24 students who study French and/or Spanish, so there are 4 who do not study either language.

5 Venn diagrams

Interpreting Venn diagrams

1 Some students were asked whether they play football (F), rugby (R), or both.

The Venn diagram shows the results.

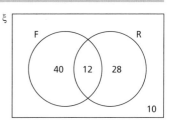

a) How many students were surveyed?

b) How many students said they only play football?

c) What is the probability that a student chosen at random plays rugby?

Drawing Venn diagrams

2 A school surveyed 100 students about how they get to school:

- 35 students take the tram (T)
- 68 students take the bus (B)
- 12 students do not take a tram or a bus.

a) Complete the Venn diagram to show these results.

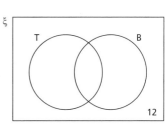

b) Work out the probability that a randomly chosen student takes the tram and the bus to school.

Collecting data

Statistics is about the collection, organisation and interpretation of data. Statistics are used to test a hypothesis in a data handling cycle.

The data handling cycle:
1. State a hypothesis, outlining the problem and planning the task.
2. Plan the data collection and collect the data.
3. Process the data using statistical calculations, e.g. mean and range (see page 132).
4. Interpret the data and make conclusions.

The final step includes reviewing the task, refining it and repeating the cycle if necessary.

The sample must be an **unbiased** sample that represents the population, e.g. randomly choosing students to ask about school dinners.

A researcher is trying to find out how many people in a town would support building a new playground. She asks parents at the gate of a local primary school.

a) Identify the population and the sample.

The population is the town and the sample is the parents at the primary school.

b) Is the sample biased? Give a reason for your answer.

Parents of young children may be more likely to support a new playground than other adults.

Yes, she is only asking people who are parents at the primary school.

c) Suggest two ways her research could be improved.

She should ask a variety of people in different areas and/or age groups, and collect a larger sample.

The different types of data

Primary data	Data that you collect
Secondary data	Data that has already been collected by someone else
Discrete data	Data that can only have certain values in a given range, e.g. the number of goals scored: 0, 1, 2, 3, and so on (it's not possible to have half a goal)
Continuous data	Data that can have any value within a given range, e.g. the height of a person: 1.83... metres
Numerical data	Data that is given as numbers, e.g. times to complete a race
Categorical data	Data that is not numerical, e.g. flavours of ice cream

Data collection terms

Survey	An organised way of collecting data; a survey could be carried out by questionnaire or by making observations in an experiment
Population	All of the group you are investigating, e.g. the students in a school
Sample	A part of the population (or group) you are investigating, e.g. 20 students from each year group
Hypothesis	An idea or assumption which is then tested to decide whether it's true or false, e.g. all students live within a 10-mile radius of the school

Processing, representing and interpreting data

To process and represent the data:
- a suitable average could be calculated (mode, median or mean)
- a suitable measure of spread could be calculated (range)
- suitable statistical charts, diagrams or graphs could be drawn.

Results are interpreted and discussed in order to make comparisons and draw conclusions, i.e. decide whether the hypothesis is true, not true or inconclusive.

Handling data

Collecting data

1 The owners of a theme park are researching visitor trends.

a) Write down whether each set of data collected from the theme park is **categorical** or **numerical**. If it is numerical, write down whether it is **discrete** or **continuous**.

i) Number of visitors per day

....

ii) Heights of the visitors

....

iii) Types of food purchased

....

iv) Queuing times for attractions

....

b) The owners want to find out which type of ride is the visitors' favourite.

Suggest how they could choose a suitable sample.

....

....

Processing, representing and interpreting data

2 The theme park owners in question 1 also decide to research how long visitors spend queuing to get into the park throughout the day.

Draw lines to match each step on the left with the correct procedure(s) on the right.

	Draw an appropriate chart, e.g. time series or bar graph.

	We think the queue times are longest between 1 pm and 2 pm.

Hypothesis	

	Look at the chart and compare the means and ranges to draw conclusions.

Plan and collect the data	

	Work out the mean and range of queuing time between each hour of the day.

Process and represent the data	

	Give visitors a card with the time they entered the queue to record the queuing time.

Interpret and discuss the results	

	Revise the hypothesis and repeat the cycle.

	Track the length of time visitors are in the queue during each hour of the day.

6 Representing data (1)

Frequency tables

A **frequency table** shows the **frequency** (i.e. the number or amount) of each group of data.

A teacher surveyed how a group of students get to school. The results were:

Walk	Walk	Cycle	Car	Cycle	Car	Walk	Cycle	Cycle
Bus	Car	Walk	Car	Car	Car	Car	Bus	Car
Cycle	Bus	Walk	Bus	Bus	Walk	Bus	Walk	

Draw a frequency table to represent this data.

	Tally	Frequency
Walk	ЈⱧⱧ ‖	7
Car	ЈⱧⱧ ‖‖	8
Bus	ЈⱧⱧ ‖	6
Cycle	ЈⱧⱧ	5

Two-way tables

A **two-way** table is a table that links two sets of information.

Draw a two-way table to show this information about people at a football match:
- Altogether there are 1200 adults.
- There are twice as many adults supporting the home team as the away team.
- Altogether there are 750 away supporters.
- There are 650 children supporting the home team.

1200 divided in the ratio 2 : 1 = 800 : 400

Fill in the numbers you are given: 1200, 750 and 650. Calculate the missing numbers. You are given the total number of adults and the ratio of adult home to adult away supporters. Once you have these, you can calculate the other missing numbers.

	Home	Away	Total
Adults	800	400	1200
Children	650	350	1000
Total	1450	750	2200

Pictograms

Pictograms can be used to represent discrete data. A **key** is needed for each symbol.

Pictogram of Hours of Sunshine

Manchester	◯ ◯ ◖
Luxor	◯ ◯ ◯ ◯ ◯ ◯
Melbourne	◯ ◖

Key: ◯ = 2 hours of sunshine

The pictogram shows the number of boys attending revision classes.

Monday	⊞ ⊞ ⊟
Tuesday	⊞ ⊞ ⊟ ▢
Wednesday	⊞ ⊞

⊞ represents 4 boys

a) How many boys attended on Monday?

10 boys

b) How many more boys attended on Tuesday than on Wednesday?

5 boys

⑥ Representing data (1)

Frequency tables

1 A shop sells these types of sandwiches in a one-hour period.

| Tuna | Ham | Beef | Tuna | Cheese | Ham | Tuna | Cheese | Cheese |
| Cheese | Beef | Ham | Cheese | Beef | Cheese | Tuna | Beef | Beef |

Complete the table.

Sandwich	Tally	Frequency
Tuna		
Cheese		
Ham		
Beef		
		Total = 18

Two-way tables

2 A hospital recorded the outcomes of patients who were treated with only physiotherapy and with only medication.

They looked at 80 patient records:
- 67 patients recovered.
- 15 patients received medication.
- $\frac{2}{3}$ of the patients who had medication recovered.

Complete the two-way table to show this information.

	Physiotherapy	Medication	Total
Recovered			67
Not recovered			
Total		15	80

Pictograms

3 The pictogram shows the results of a student survey of favourite after-school clubs.

a) How many students were surveyed?

Football	◯ ◯ ◯
Gymnastics	◯ ◯ ◖
Dance	◯ ◯ ◯ ◯
Swimming	◯ ◯
Drama	◯ ◯ ◖
	◯ = 8 students

....

b) Which activity is the most popular?

....

c) Which **two** activities do an equal number of students prefer?

.... and ....

Representing data (2)

Pie charts

A **pie chart** is a circle divided into sectors to show the proportion of different categories that make up the whole. You may have to compare two pie charts.

> The largest sector in a pie chart is the mode (see page 132).

To draw a pie chart:
1. Divide the frequency of each group by the total frequency. Multiply by 360°.
2. Draw a circle. Measure each sector using the angles from your calculations. Measure each angle from the base line of the previous sector.
3. Label each sector.

To work out frequencies from a pie chart:
1. Divide 360° by the the total frequency represented by the pie chart to find how many degrees per item.
2. Divide the angle of each sector by the value from step 1 to find the frequency of each sector.

The table (below left) shows data about the favourite holiday destinations of some students.

Draw a pie chart to represent the data. | Divide each frequency by the total frequency and multiply by 360°.

Favourite holiday	Number of students
UK	7
France	3
Spain	8
Total	18

Calculation	Angle
$\frac{7}{18} \times 360°$	140°
$\frac{3}{18} \times 360°$	60°
$\frac{8}{18} \times 360°$	160°
Total = 360°	

Favourite Holiday

The angles must sum to 360°.

Bar charts and vertical line charts

A **bar chart** (for categorical data) or a **vertical line graph** (for discrete data) can display frequencies.

A **multiple bar chart** can be used to compare two or more groups of data side by side.

> The height (or length) of the lines or bars shows the frequency of each group.

The table shows the number of tries scored by a rugby team in 12 games. Draw a vertical line graph to show the data.

Number of tries scored	0	1	2	3	4
Frequency	4	1	4	1	2

Draw the lines up to the frequency in the table.

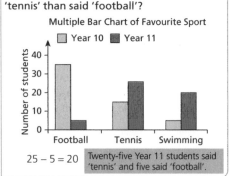

Vertical Line Graph of Tries

This bar chart shows the favourite sports of some Year 10 and Year 11 students.

How many more Year 11 students said 'tennis' than said 'football'?

Multiple Bar Chart of Favourite Sport

$25 - 5 = 20$ | Twenty-five Year 11 students said 'tennis' and five said 'football'.

Representing data (2)

Pie charts

1 Here is some data about the favourite genre of books of students at a school.

Work out the angle you would need to draw for each sector.

Genre of book	Number of students	Angle (°)
Non-fiction	108	
Fantasy	162	
Mystery	270	
Historical fiction	324	
General fiction	216	
Total		

Bar charts and vertical line charts

2 Draw a bar chart showing the data from question 1.

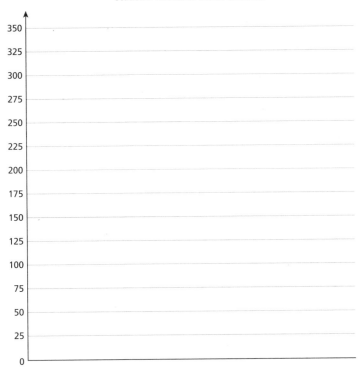

Students' Favourite Genre of Books

Measures of central tendency and spread

Mode, median, mean and range

An **average** is a measure used to represent a set of data. The most commonly used averages are:
- the **mode**, which is the most common value
- the **median**, which is the middle value of the ordered data
- the **mean** = $\frac{\text{sum of all the values}}{\text{total number of values}}$

The **range** is the biggest value – smallest value.

Take the data 4, 0, 2, 3, 5, 2, 2, 6, 3.

The mode is 2.

The median is 3 (0 2 2 2 ③ 3 4 5 6)

The mean is $\frac{0+2+2+2+3+3+4+5+6}{9} = \frac{27}{9} = 3$

The range is 6 – 0 = 6

> Mean, median and mode are **measures of central tendency**. Range is a **measure of spread**.

Use the frequency table (below left) to work out the mode, median, mean and range of the number of pets per family.

No. of pets (x)	Frequency (f)
0	4
1	6
2	9
3	1
	Total = 20

Mode is 2 pets.

Median is the middle of the 20 values (halfway between the circled 10th and 11th values).

Median = 1.5 pets

Mean is $\frac{27}{20} = 1.35$ pets

Range is 3 – 0 = 3 pets

Listing in order:
0, 0, 0, 0, 1, 1,
1, 1, 1, ⓵ ⓶ 2,
2, 2, 2, 2, 2,
2, 2, 3

Sum of values (fx) ÷ number of values (f)

	fx
	$0 \times 4 = 0$
	$1 \times 6 = 6$
	$2 \times 9 = 18$
	$3 \times 1 = 3$
	Total = 27

Mode, median and mean from a grouped frequency table

It is not possible to find the exact values from a grouped frequency table. Instead, you can work out the class that contains the mode (the **modal class**) and the class that contains the median. You can find an estimate of the mean but you can't work out the range as the exact highest and lowest values are unknown.

To estimate the mean:
1. Find the midpoint of the class intervals.
2. Multiply the frequency by the midpoint of each class interval, $f \times x$. Work out the total of $f \times x$.
3. Work out the total frequency.
4. Estimate the mean using $\frac{\text{sum of } f \times x}{\text{sum of } f}$

The grouped frequency table shows the recorded temperatures for 24 days.

Recorded temp., T (°C)	Frequency (f)
$10 \leqslant T < 15$	2
$15 \leqslant T < 20$	4
$20 \leqslant T < 25$	5
$25 \leqslant T < 30$	8
$30 \leqslant T < 35$	5
	Total = 24

a) Write down the modal class.

$25°C \leqslant T < 30°C$ ◄ The class with highest frequency.

b) Work out the class that contains the median.

$25°C \leqslant T < 30°C$ There are 24 values, so the median is between the 12th and 13th values. These are in $25°C \leqslant T < 30°C$ (which contains the 12th to 19th values).

c) Calculate an estimate for the mean of the recorded temperatures.

Midpoint (x)	fx
12.5	$2 \times 12.5 = 25$
17.5	$4 \times 17.5 = 70$
22.5	$5 \times 22.5 = 112.5$
27.5	$8 \times 27.5 = 220$
32.5	$5 \times 32.5 = 162.5$
	Total = 590

These are halfway values for the class intervals.

Estimate of the mean = $\frac{\text{sum of } f \times x}{\text{sum of } f}$

$= \frac{590}{24} = 24.6°C$ (1 d.p.)

Measures of central tendency and spread

Mode, median, mean and range

1 Here is a set of data:

x	Frequency, f
3	1
4	9
5	6
6	3

Work out the following for the data, giving your answers to 2 decimal places where appropriate. You may add columns to the table to help you.

a) Mode

b) Mean

c) Median

d) Range

Mode, median and mean from a grouped frequency table

2 Here is a set of data:

Class	Frequency, f
$0 < x \leqslant 2$	10
$2 < x \leqslant 4$	21
$4 < x \leqslant 6$	13
$6 < x \leqslant 8$	7

Work out the following for the data, giving your answers to 2 decimal places where appropriate. You may add columns to the table to help you.

a) The modal class

b) The class that contains the median

c) An estimate of the mean

Scatter graphs and time series

Scatter graphs

A **scatter graph** helps to compare two sets of data on the same pair of axes. **Correlation** describes any trend shown.

Correlation means the two values share some sort of relationship, it does not mean that one value causes the other. Correlation is not causation.

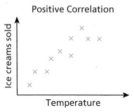

Positive Correlation

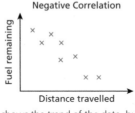

Negative Correlation

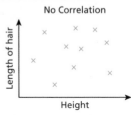

No Correlation

A **line of best fit** is a straight line that shows the trend of the data, but it doesn't have to pass exactly through any of the points. It can be used to estimate unknown values **within** the range of the points plotted. Correlation is 'strong' if all points lie very close to the line of best fit and 'weak' if they are more spread.

The table shows how much money a company spent on advertising and the revenue generated.

Advertising spend (£k)	10	15	20	25	30	35	40	45	55
Revenue generated (£k)	50	70	75	90	130	160	50	180	220

a) Draw a scatter graph to show the data.

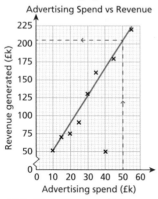

b) What type of correlation is shown?

As the advertising spend increases, the revenue generated increases.

The graph shows a positive correlation.

c) Estimate the revenue generated if the company spends £50 000 on advertising.

Add a line of best fit (shown by the red line) and use it for estimation (as shown by the dashed lines).

If the company spends £50 000, it will generate approximately £205 000 in revenue.

d) Identify the outlier in this data.

Outliers are any points that do not fit the trend.

The data point (40, 50) is the outlier.

Time series graphs

A **time series graph** (a **line graph**) can be used for discrete or continuous data to show change over time.

The table shows data about temperatures at different times of the day.

Time	10 am	11 am	Noon	1 pm	2 pm
Temp. (°C)	11°C	12°C	13°C	14°C	12°C

Draw a time series graph to show the data.

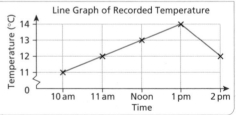

Scatter graphs and time series

Scatter graphs

1 The scatter graph shows the maximum daily temperature and the number of ice creams sold at a park over a period of 14 days.

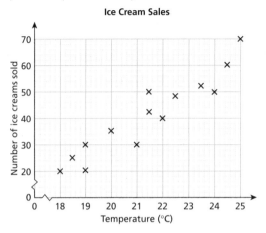

Ice Cream Sales

a) Draw a line of best fit on the graph.

b) Use the line of best fit to estimate the number of ice creams sold if the temperature is 23°C. ....

Time series graphs

2 The number of ice creams sold each day for a week at another park was recorded in this table.

Day	Mon	Tue	Wed	Thu	Fri	Sat	Sun
Ice creams sold	10	15	8	12	27	38	34

Draw a time series graph to show the data.

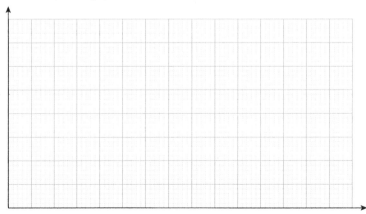

Mixed questions

1 A sequence is made using patterns of sticks.

1   2   3

a) Draw the next pattern in the sequence.

b) Work out the number of sticks in pattern 10.

....

c) Andrew says there is a pattern with 84 sticks in it.

Explain why he must be wrong.

....

....

2 a) Simplify $x + 2x + 4x$

....

b) Work out the value of $3x + 5y$ when $x = 8$ and $y = -4$

....

c) Solve $3x - 2 = 16$

$x =$ ....

d) Solve $4(2x + 5) = -28$

$x =$ ....

3 Here is a list of numbers:

6	9	13	15	18	20	27

From the list, write down:

a) a square number ....   b) a prime number ....

c) the factors of 45 ....   d) the multiples of 9 ....

Mixed questions

4 a) Complete the table of values for $y = 3x - 4$

x	−1	0	1	2	3
y	−7		−1		5

b) Draw the graph of $y = 3x - 4$ on the grid below for values from $x = -1$ to $x = 3$.

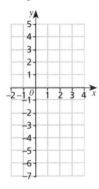

5 Shape A is shown on the coordinate grid.

a) Reflect shape A in the line $y = -1$.
Label the image as shape B.

b) Translate shape B by the vector $\begin{pmatrix} -5 \\ 1 \end{pmatrix}$.
Label the image as shape C.

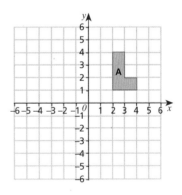

6 a) Factorise $x^2 + 7x + 12$

b) Solve $x^2 + 7x = -12$

$x = $ .... or $x = $ ....

Mixed questions

Calculator allowed questions

7 Mateo is buying a new refrigerator and sees offers from three shops.

FRIDGE WORLD

$\frac{1}{3}$ off usual price of **£810**

FRIDGE BARGAINS

■■ PAY DEPOSIT OF £100 ■■
Then pay 12 equal instalments of £40

The Electric Store

£500
plus
20% VAT

Mateo wants to pay as little as possible.

From which shop should he buy the refrigerator? Show your working.

_____

_____

_____

_____

8 Hiram deposits £2500 into a savings account, earning 3% interest compounded annually.

Work out the amount in his account after 3 years.

£ ....

9 Work out the area of the trapezium.

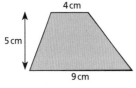

4 cm

5 cm

9 cm

.... cm²

10

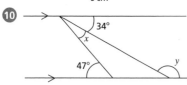

34°

x

47°

y

a) Work out the size of angle x.

x = ... °

b) Work out the size of angle y.

y = ... °

Mixed questions

11 A semicircle is shown.

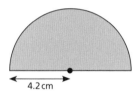

4.2 cm

a) Work out the area of the semicircle. Give your answer to 2 decimal places.

....cm²

b) Work out the perimeter of the semicircle. Give your answer to 2 decimal places.

....cm

12 20 students were asked to name their favourite sport. Here are the results:

Football	Cricket	Rugby	Swimming	Football
Football	Cricket	Rugby	Football	Cricket
Rugby	Rugby	Swimming	Football	Rugby
Football	Football	Cricket	Rugby	Cricket

a) Complete the table to show these results.

Favourite sport	Tally	Frequency
Football		
Cricket		
Rugby		
Swimming		

b) Which sport was chosen by the greatest number of students? ....

c) Show the results on a bar chart.

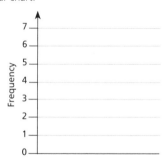

Mixed questions

13 Two similar trapeziums are shown below.

Work out the length of the side labelled x.

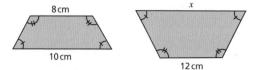

8 cm

10 cm

x

12 cm

$x =$ .... cm

14 The coin is flipped and the spinner is spun.

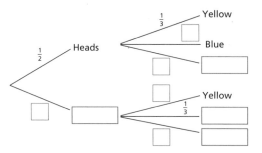

$\frac{1}{2}$ / Heads

$\frac{1}{3}$ / Yellow

Blue

Yellow

$\frac{1}{3}$

a) Complete the tree diagram to show the possible outcomes.

b) Work out the probability that the coin lands on tails and the spinner lands on yellow.

....

15 This scatter graph shows the number of driving tests taken to pass and the number of hours of lessons for 13 students.

a) One of the students had more hours than normal for the number of tests taken.

Circle this point on the graph and give a reason why it should be ignored.

....

....

b) Draw a line of best fit on the graph.

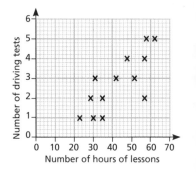

c) Describe the relationship between the number of tests taken to pass and the number of hours of lessons.

....

....

Mixed questions

16 Here is a right-angled triangle:

a) Work out the length of the side labelled x.

$x =$ _____ cm

b) Work out the size of angle a.
Give your answer to the nearest degree.

$a =$ _____ °

17 Theo raises £1300 and divides it in the ratio of 3 : 2 between a panda charity and an elephant charity.

How much money does each charity receive?

Pandas: £_____

Elephants: £_____

18 a) Work out the surface area of the shape.

_____ cm²

b) Work out the volume of the shape.

_____ cm³

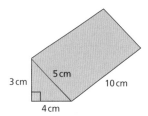

19 Show that these two triangles are congruent.

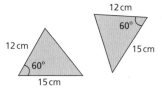

_____

_____

Key facts and vocabulary

Number

Adding and subtracting fractions	1. Rewrite the problem using equivalent fractions with a common denominator. 2. Add or subtract the numerators. Keep the denominator the same. 3. Simplify if possible.	Work out $2\frac{2}{3} + 1\frac{1}{2}$ $2\frac{2}{3} + 1\frac{1}{2} = 2 + 1 + \frac{2}{3} + \frac{1}{2}$ $= 3 + \frac{4}{6} + \frac{3}{6}$ ← $\frac{2}{3} = \frac{4}{6}$ and $\frac{1}{2} = \frac{3}{6}$ $= 3 + 1\frac{1}{6}$ ← $\frac{4}{6} + \frac{3}{6} = \frac{7}{6} = 1\frac{1}{6}$ $= 4\frac{1}{6}$
Calculations in standard form	To calculate in standard form: 1. Change the numbers to ordinary form. 2. Complete the calculation. 3. Change the numbers back to standard form if required.	$(1.328 \times 10^3) + (2.7 \times 10^2) =$ $1.328 \times 10^3 = 1328$ $2.7 \times 10^2 = 270$ $1328 + 270 = 1598$ $1598 = 1.598 \times 10^3$
Multiplying and dividing fractions	To multiply fractions, multiply the numerators together and multiply the denominators together. To divide fractions, remember KFC.	**Keep the first fraction as it is** **Flip the second fraction** **Change ÷ to ×**
Multiplying and dividing negative numbers	$+ \times + = +$ $+ \div + = +$ $- \times + = -$ $- \div + = -$ $+ \times - = -$ $+ \div - = -$ $- \times - = +$ $- \div - = +$	
Negative numbers	Increasing → −10 −9 −8 −7 −6 −5 −4 −3 −2 −1 0 1 2 3 4 5 6 7 8 9 10 ← Decreasing	
Order of operations	# B I D M A S ( ) x^2 ÷ or × + or −	
Prime	Prime numbers have exactly two factors: 1 and itself. 1 is not a prime number.	
Prime factor decomposition	A process for breaking down a number into its prime factors.	90 9 10 $90 = 2 \times 3^2 \times 5$ ③ ③ ② ⑤
Root	Inverse of a power	$3^2 = 9$, so $\sqrt{9} = 3$ Square root of 9 is 3. $3^3 = 27$, so $\sqrt[3]{27} = 3$ Cube root of 27 is 3.
Rounding to significant figures	4852 rounded to 1 s.f. is 5000 4852 rounded to 2 s.f. is 4900	0.00649 rounded to 1 s.f. is 0.006 0.00649 rounded to 2 s.f. is 0.0065
Simplifying	Simplify fractions and ratios by dividing both numbers by common factors.	÷3 $\frac{9}{15} = \frac{3}{5}$ $÷3 \left(\begin{matrix} 9 : 3 \\ 3 : 1 \end{matrix} \right) ÷3$ ÷3

Key facts and vocabulary

Algebra

Arithmetic sequence	Terms go up or down by the same amount (common difference) each time. 2, 5, 8, 11, 14, … Common difference +3 5, 3, 1, –1, –3, … Common difference –2
Cubic functions	Cubic functions have an x^3 term as the highest power of x, e.g. $y = x^3$ or $y = x^3 - 4$. The general shape of a cubic function is:
Continuing a sequence from pictures	To continue a sequence from pictures, find the pattern and draw the required terms. To draw the next term in this sequence, note that three more 'sticks' are added each time to create an additional rhombus.
Equation of a straight line	$y = mx + c$ where m is the gradient and c is the y-intercept
Expanding or multiplying out a single set of brackets	Multiply every term inside the bracket by the term outside the bracket. $3(x + 4) = 3x + 12$ $5(2y - 1) = 10y - 5$
Expanding or multiplying out two sets of brackets	Multiply every term in the first bracket by every term in the second bracket.
Factorising	Writing an expression as a multiplication.

Key facts and vocabulary

Working out the equation of a line	1. Find two points on the line. 2. Find the gradient between them. 3. Find the y-intercept. 4. Write the equation using $y = mx + c$. $m = \frac{7-5}{2-1} = 2$ y-intercept is 3 Equation is $y = 2x + 3$
Geometric sequence	Each term is multiplied by the same number to get the next term. 2, 4, 8, 16, 32, ... Each term is multiplied by 2 1000, 100, 10, 1, 0.1, ... Each term is multiplied by 0.1
Gradient	Measure of the steepness of a line. Positive gradient Negative gradient Gradient = 0 Gradient = $\frac{\text{change in } y}{\text{change in } x}$ change in y change in x

Laws of indices		
To multiply powers of the same base, add the powers	$a^m \times a^n = a^{(m+n)}$
To divide powers of the same base, subtract the powers	$a^m \div a^n = a^{(m-n)}$
To raise a power to another power, multiply the powers	$(a^m)^n = a^{(m \times n)}$
Any base to the power of 1 is itself	$a^1 = a$
Any base to the power of 0 is 1	$a^0 = 1$
A negative power means the reciprocal of the power	$a^{-m} = \frac{1}{a^m}$

Midpoint of a line segment	Midpoint = $\left(\frac{x_1 + x_2}{2}, \frac{y_1 + y_2}{2}\right)$ To find the midpoint of the line segment shown: Midpoint = $\left(\frac{3 + (-1)}{2}, \frac{2 + 4}{2}\right)$ $= (1, 3)$ $(-1, 4)$ $(3, 2)$

Key facts and vocabulary

Parallel lines	Lines that stay the same distance apart and never intersect. 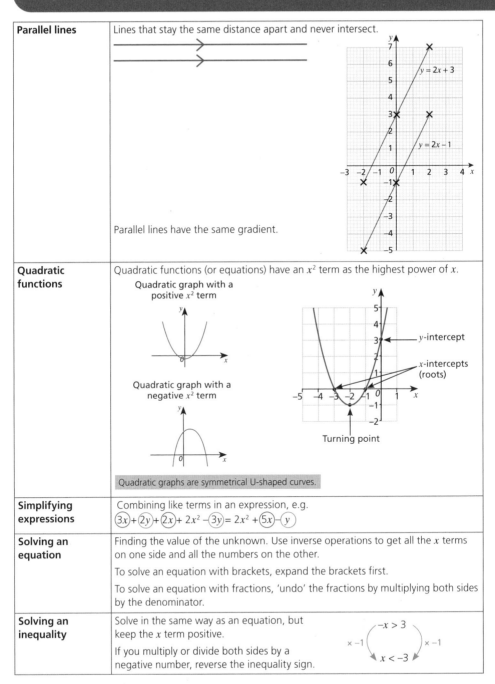 Parallel lines have the same gradient.
Quadratic functions	Quadratic functions (or equations) have an x^2 term as the highest power of x. Quadratic graphs are symmetrical U-shaped curves.
Simplifying expressions	Combining like terms in an expression, e.g. $(3x) + (2y) + (2x) + 2x^2 - (3y) = 2x^2 + (5x) - (y)$
Solving an equation	Finding the value of the unknown. Use inverse operations to get all the x terms on one side and all the numbers on the other. To solve an equation with brackets, expand the brackets first. To solve an equation with fractions, 'undo' the fractions by multiplying both sides by the denominator.
Solving an inequality	Solve in the same way as an equation, but keep the x term positive. If you multiply or divide both sides by a negative number, reverse the inequality sign. $-x > 3$ $\times -1 \quad \times -1$ $x < -3$

Key facts and vocabulary

Solving simultaneous equations using graphs	Plot the graphs of the two equations. The solutions are the x- and y-values where the two lines cross $x = 1$, $y = 7$	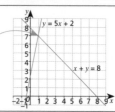

Ratio, proportion and rates of change

Compound interest	Interest that is earned on the balance and on the interest, in contrast to simple interest which is only earned on the original balance. To work out compound interest: **1.** Substitute the given values into the formula $A = P\left(1 + \frac{r}{100}\right)^n$ **2.** Work out the value needed.
Compound measures	A compound measure or compound unit is a measure of one quantity in relation to another, e.g. speed. $\begin{array}{c}\text{Distance}\\\hline \text{Speed} \mid \text{Time}\end{array}$
Direct proportion	As one quantity increases, the other quantity increases at the same rate, e.g. when x doubles, y doubles. $y = kx$ k is a constant (a number that does not change)
Dividing into a given ratio	**1.** Count the total parts of the ratio. **2.** Divide the quantity by the total parts to find the value of one part. **3.** Multiply by each part.
Working out a missing amount in a ratio	**1.** Divide the given amount by the given number of parts to find the value of one part. **2.** Multiply the part corresponding to the unknown value by the result of step 1.
Inverse proportion	As one quantity increases, the other quantity decreases at the same rate, e.g. when x doubles, y halves. $y = \frac{k}{x}$ k is a constant
Multiplier	The decimal value used to work out a percentage change. To increase by 20%, the multiplier is 1.2 To decrease by 20%, the multiplier is 0.8
Proportion	A proportion is a comparison of a part to a whole. Two values are in direct proportion if the ratio between them remains fixed as the values change, e.g. the number of miles travelled when driving at a constant speed.

Key facts and vocabulary

Percentage change	Percentage change = $\frac{\text{amount of increase or decrease}}{\text{original value}} \times 100$ Repeated percentage change: New value = original value × multiplier^x (where x is the number of changes)
Ratio	Compares two or more quantities and is written with a colon (:) between each value. The ratio of red to blue beads is 5 : 3
Reverse percentages	Working backwards to find the original amount. Divide by the multiplier.
Unit ratio	A ratio written in the form 1 : n or n : 1. It can be used to compare ratios.

Geometry and measures

Arc	Part of the circumference of a circle. Length of an arc = $\frac{\text{angle at centre}}{360°}$ × circumference of circle Circumference → Arc
Area of a circle	$A = \pi r^2$
Area of a parallelogram	Area of a parallelogram = base × perpendicular height $$A = bh$$
Area of a trapezium	$A = \frac{1}{2}(a + b)h$
Area of a triangle	Area of triangle = $\frac{1}{2}$ × base × perpendicular height $$A = \frac{1}{2}bh$$
Bearing	A three-digit angle measurement to show the direction of one place to another, starting North and measuring clockwise, e.g. 030°, 120°, 348°.
Circumference of a circle	$C = 2\pi r$ $C = \pi d$ Diameter (d) Radius (r) Circumference

Key facts and vocabulary

Congruent	Congruent shapes are exactly the same shape and size. Two triangles are congruent if one or more of these four criteria are true:

Side, Side, Side (SSS)	Side, Angle, Side (SAS)	Angle, Side, Angle (ASA) or Angle, Angle, Side (AAS)	Right angle, Hypotenuse, Side (RHS)

Enlargement	An enlargement multiplies: • each length on the shape by the scale factor • the distance from the centre by the scale factor. To describe an enlargement: Enlargement scale factor ...., centre .... number point
Exterior and interior angles	Sum of interior angles in a polygon = (number of sides − 2) × 180° Sum of exterior angles in a polygon = 360° Interior angle + exterior angle = 180° Exterior angle Interior angle
Pythagoras' theorem	$a^2 + b^2 = c^2$ b c ← c is the length of the hypotenuse a a and b are the lengths of the two shorter sides
Rotation	A rotation turns a shape around a point, called the centre of rotation. Use tracing paper. To describe a rotation: Rotation ....° clockwise/anticlockwise, centre .... angle direction point
Scale factor	The value by which all side lengths are multiplied in an enlargement. A to B: enlargement scale factor 2 B to A: enlargement scale factor $\frac{1}{2}$ 2×2 A B $6 \times \frac{1}{2}$
Sector	The area of a circle enclosed by two radii and the arc between them.

Key facts and vocabulary

Similar	Similar shapes are enlargements of each other: • The angles in each shape are the same. • They have the same shape but different sizes. • Each side length in the enlarged shape has been multiplied by the same scale factor. X Y
Surface area	The total area of all the faces of a 3D shape.
Translation	A translation slides a shape across a grid. Translation 4 squares right, 2 down. To describe a translation, a column vector can be used: $\begin{pmatrix} 4 \\ -2 \end{pmatrix}$ ← Movement right/left (a negative value means 'left') ← Movement up/down (a negative value means 'down') Object Image
Trigonometric ratios	$\sin \theta = \dfrac{\text{opposite}}{\text{hypotenuse}} = \dfrac{\text{opp}}{\text{hyp}}$ $\cos \theta = \dfrac{\text{adjacent}}{\text{hypotenuse}} = \dfrac{\text{adj}}{\text{hyp}}$ $\tan \theta = \dfrac{\text{opposite}}{\text{adjacent}} = \dfrac{\text{opp}}{\text{adj}}$ opposite (to angle θ) hypotenuse adjacent (to angle θ) You can remember these using: **S O H** **C A H** **T O A** $\sin = \dfrac{\text{opp}}{\text{hyp}}$ $\cos = \dfrac{\text{adj}}{\text{hyp}}$ $\tan = \dfrac{\text{opp}}{\text{adj}}$
Vector	A line segment of a certain length and a particular direction. Vector $\overrightarrow{AB} = \mathbf{a} = \begin{pmatrix} 3 \\ -4 \end{pmatrix}$ A 3 −4 a B
Volume of a cone	Volume of a cone $= \dfrac{1}{3} \times \pi r^2 h$ h r
Volume of a cylinder	Volume of a cylinder $= \pi \times r^2 \times h$ r h

Key facts and vocabulary

Volume of a prism	Volume of a prism = area of cross-section × length, where the cross-section is the 2D shape made when cutting through the prism
Volume of a pyramid	Volume of a pyramid = $\frac{1}{3}$ × area of base × vertical height
Volume of a sphere	Volume of a sphere = $\frac{4}{3}\pi r^3$

Probability

Expected result	Expected result = P(event) × number of trials For rolling a dice 30 times, expected number of 3s = $\frac{1}{6}$ × 30 = 5
Independent events	The result of one event does not change the probability of the second event, e.g. for a dice, rolling a 6 does not change the probability of rolling a 6 next time.
Mutually exclusive	Two events that cannot occur at the same time. The probabilities of all the mutually exclusive events in a trial add up to 1. For this spinner, P(Y) + P(G) + P(R) + P(B) = 1
Outcome	The result of a probability experiment or trial, e.g. for the experiment 'rolling a dice', possible outcomes are 1, 2, 3, 4, 5 or 6.
Probability of an event	P(event) = $\frac{\text{number of ways the outcome can occur}}{\text{total number of possible outcomes}}$ For this spinner, P(R) = $\frac{1}{4}$
Probability of an event not happening	P(event not happening) = 1 − P(event happening) For this spinner, P(not blue) = 1 − P(blue)
Probability of combined independent events	The product rule of independent events is P(A and B) = P(A) × P(B)
Relative frequency	Relative frequency = $\frac{\text{number of times event occurred}}{\text{total number of trials}}$ The greater the number of trials, the closer the relative frequency gets to the theoretical probability.

Key facts and vocabulary

Sample space	Set of all possible outcomes, e.g. for the experiment 'rolling a dice', the sample space is 1, 2, 3, 4, 5, 6.
	A sample space for two combined events can be shown in a two-way table.
Theoretical probability	Probability you calculate using this formula:
	$P(\text{event}) = \dfrac{\text{number of ways the outcome can occur}}{\text{total number of possible outcomes}}$
Tree diagram	To work out the probability of combined events, multiply the probability of the outcomes along each branch. The probabilities on each pair of branches should sum to 1. 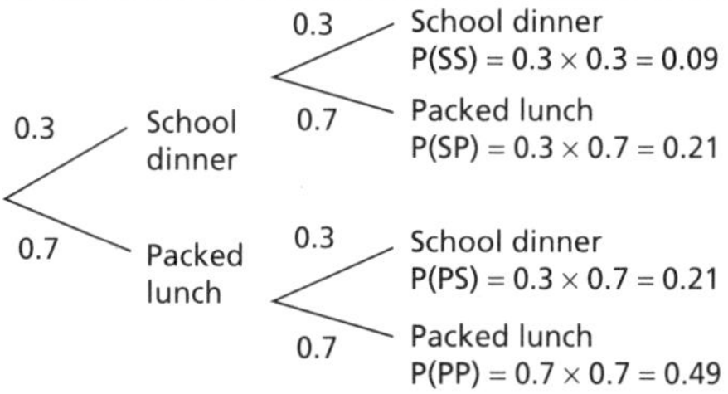

Tree diagram labels:

0.3 — School dinner
0.3 School dinner
0.7 Packed lunch — P(SS) = 0.3 × 0.3 = 0.09
Packed lunch P(SP) = 0.3 × 0.7 = 0.21
0.7 Packed lunch
0.3 School dinner P(PS) = 0.3 × 0.7 = 0.21
0.7 Packed lunch P(PP) = 0.7 × 0.7 = 0.49

Venn diagram	A diagram showing the relationship between two or more things.
	This Venn diagram shows whether students had cereal, eggs, both, or neither for breakfast.

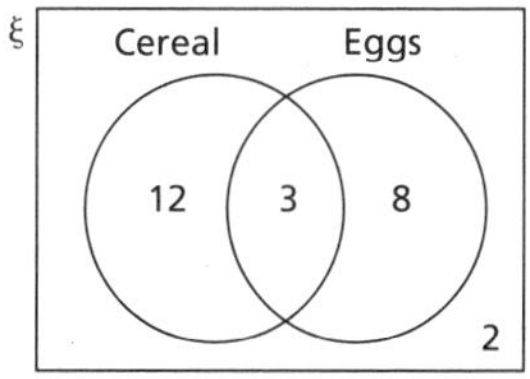

Venn diagram: ξ Cereal Eggs 12 3 8 2

Statistics

Categorical data	Data that is not numerical, e.g. favourite colours.
Continuous data	Data that can have any value within a given range, e.g. the weight of a person: 73.2… kg
Discrete data	Data that can only have certain values in a given range, e.g. the number of students in a school will always be an integer value (it's not possible to have a quarter of a student or half of a student).
Estimating the mean from a grouped frequency table	1. Find the midpoint of the class intervals. 2. Multiply the frequency by the midpoint of each class interval, $f \times x$. 3. Work out the total of $f \times x$. 4. Work out the total frequency. 5. Estimate the mean using $\dfrac{\text{sum of } f \times x}{\text{sum of } f}$
Mean	$\text{Mean} = \dfrac{\text{Total sum of values}}{\text{Number of values}}$
Median	Middle value when values are in order. In a set of n values, the median is the $\frac{n+1}{2}$th value.
Mode	Most common value; the value with highest frequency.
Numerical data	Data that is given as numbers, e.g. test scores.
Range	Range = highest value – lowest value

Key facts and vocabulary

Pie chart	A circular chart that shows the proportion of different groups that make up a whole. To draw a pie chart: **1.** Divide the frequency of each group by the total frequency. Multiply by 360°. **2.** Draw a circle. Measure each sector using the angles from your calculations. Measure each angle from the base line of the previous sector. **3.** Label each sector. To compare two pie charts, look at the corresponding sections. These two pie charts show that a higher proportion of people in Town A enjoy playing football than in Town B. A higher proportion of people in Town B enjoy tennis than in Town A. Without numbers, you can't tell if more people play tennis in Town B or Town A. 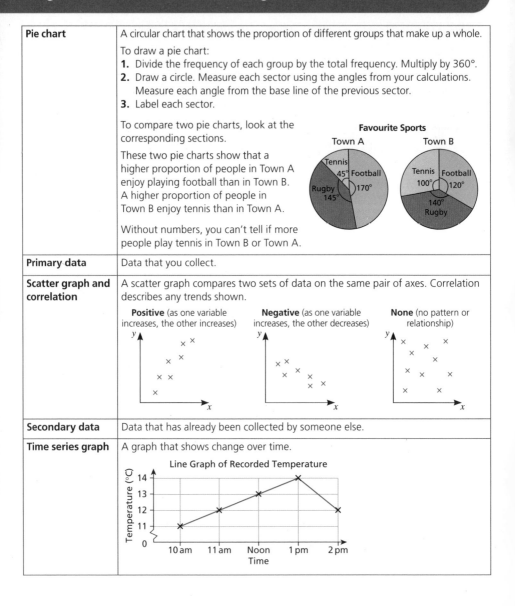
Primary data	Data that you collect.
Scatter graph and correlation	A scatter graph compares two sets of data on the same pair of axes. Correlation describes any trends shown. **Positive** (as one variable increases, the other increases) **Negative** (as one variable increases, the other decreases) **None** (no pattern or relationship)
Secondary data	Data that has already been collected by someone else.
Time series graph	A graph that shows change over time.

Answers

Page 7

1.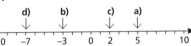

2. a) -7 b) 9

   c) -2 d) -2

3. a) 12 b) -18

   c) -6 d) 3

Page 9

1. a) 781 b) 1835

   c) 82 d) 1246

2. a) $16\,170$ b) 1246

   c) 9361 d) 1833

3. a) 82 b) 283

   c) 53 d) 220.5

Page 11

1. $\frac{16}{20} = \frac{8}{10} = \frac{40}{50} = \frac{4}{5}$

2. a) $\frac{2}{5}$ b) $\frac{3}{7}$ c) $\frac{3}{4}$ d) $3\frac{2}{9}$

3. a) $3\frac{1}{4} = \frac{(4 \times 3) + 1}{4} = \frac{13}{4}$

   b) $2\frac{5}{8} = \frac{(8 \times 2) + 5}{8} = \frac{21}{8}$

4. a) $\frac{18}{5} = 3\frac{3}{5}$ ($18 \div 5 = 3$ remainder 3)

   b) $\frac{21}{8} = 2\frac{5}{8}$ ($21 \div 8 = 2$ remainder 5)

5. a) $\frac{3}{5} + \frac{2}{10} = \frac{6}{10} + \frac{2}{10} = \frac{8}{10} = \frac{4}{5}$

   b) $\frac{2}{3} + \frac{5}{8} = \frac{16}{24} + \frac{15}{24} = \frac{31}{24} = 1\frac{7}{24}$

   c) $3\frac{1}{3} + 4\frac{3}{4} = 3 + 4 + \frac{4}{12} + \frac{9}{12} = 7 + \frac{13}{12} = 8\frac{1}{12}$

   d) $2\frac{3}{8} + 1\frac{1}{2} = 2 + 1 + \frac{3}{8} + \frac{4}{8} = 3\frac{7}{8}$

6. a) $\frac{5}{7} - \frac{3}{14} = \frac{10}{14} - \frac{3}{14} = \frac{7}{14} = \frac{1}{2}$

   b) $\frac{4}{5} - \frac{1}{8} = \frac{32}{40} - \frac{5}{40} = \frac{27}{40}$

   c) $3\frac{1}{2} - 2\frac{1}{3} = \frac{7}{2} - \frac{7}{3} = \frac{21}{6} - \frac{14}{6} = \frac{7}{6} = 1\frac{1}{6}$

   d) $5\frac{2}{3} - 3\frac{1}{8} = 5 - 3 + \frac{2}{3} - \frac{1}{8} = 2 + \frac{16}{24} - \frac{3}{24} = 2\frac{13}{24}$

7. $\frac{5}{8}$ of a litre

Page 13

1. a) $\frac{2}{3} \times \frac{5}{8} = \frac{2 \times 5}{3 \times 8} = \frac{10}{24} = \frac{5}{12}$

   b) $2\frac{1}{3} \times 3\frac{3}{4} = \frac{7}{3} \times \frac{15}{4} = \frac{105}{12} = 8\frac{9}{12} = 8\frac{3}{4}$

   c) $1\frac{3}{8} \times 2\frac{1}{4} = \frac{11}{8} \times \frac{9}{4} = \frac{99}{32} = 3\frac{3}{32}$

2. a) $\frac{3}{4} \div \frac{1}{3} = \frac{3}{4} \times \frac{3}{1} = \frac{9}{4} = 2\frac{1}{4}$

   b) $\frac{4}{7} \div \frac{3}{5} = \frac{4}{7} \times \frac{5}{3} = \frac{20}{21}$

   c) $2\frac{2}{5} \div 1\frac{1}{8} = \frac{12}{5} \div \frac{9}{8} = \frac{12}{5} \times \frac{8}{9} = \frac{96}{45} = \frac{32}{15} = 2\frac{2}{15}$

   d) $3\frac{3}{4} \div \frac{2}{3} = \frac{15}{4} \times \frac{3}{2} = \frac{45}{8} = 5\frac{5}{8}$

3. a) $\frac{1}{3} \times 30 = 30 \div 3 = 10$

   b) $\frac{3}{8} \times 24 = (24 \div 8) \times 3 = 3 \times 3 = 9$

4. a) $1\,\text{m} = 100\,\text{cm}$, so $\frac{15}{100} = \frac{3}{20}$

   b) $1\,\text{g} = 1000\,\text{mg}$, so $\frac{30}{15\,000} = \frac{1}{500}$

5. $1 - \frac{3}{5} = \frac{2}{5}$ of the students took packed lunch.

   $\frac{2}{5} \times 30 = (30 \div 5) \times 2 = 12$

Page 15

1. $0.588, 0.805, 0.85, 8.05, 8.5$

2. a) 20.29 b) 53.28

3. a) 47.12 b) 38.221

4. a) 7.1 b) 96

5. a) $0.512 = \frac{512}{1000} = \frac{64}{125}$

   b) $\frac{5}{8} = 5 \div 8 = 0.625$

Page 17

1. a) 12 b) 10 c) 60 d) 15

2. a) 4 b) 8 c) 3 d) 4

Page 19

1. a) $61, 83$

   b) $18, 39, 54$

   c) $16, 49$

2. a) $2 \times 2 \times 2 \times 2 \times 2 = 2^5$

   b) $2 \times 2 \times 2 \times 5 = 2^3 \times 5$

   c) $2 \times 3 \times 3 = 2 \times 3^2$

   d) $2 \times 2 \times 2 \times 3 \times 5 = 2^3 \times 3 \times 5$

3. a) There are three 2s in common
so HCF $= 2 \times 2 \times 2 = 8$

   b) There are two 2s and one 5 left
so LCM $= 8 \times 2 \times 2 \times 5 = 160$

Page 21

1. a) $3 \times 3 = 9$

   b) $6 \times 6 = 36$

   c) $10 \times 10 \times 10 \times 10 = 10\,000$

2. a) 64

  b) 625

  c) 5832

3. a) $3^4 \times 3^7 = 3^{4+7} = 3^{11}$

  b) $\frac{4^8}{4^2} = 4^{8-2} = 4^6$

  c) $(5^2)^8 = 5^{2 \times 8} = 5^{16}$

  d) $\frac{(7^2 \times 7^6)}{7^3} = \frac{7^{2+6}}{7^3} = \frac{7^8}{7^3} = 7^{8-3} = 7^5$

4. a) $\sqrt{49} = 7$

  b) $\sqrt{196} = 14$

  c) $\sqrt[3]{125} = 5$

5. $\sqrt{81} = 9$ and $\sqrt{100} = 10$ so $\sqrt{87}$ lies between 9 and 10

Page 23

1. a) 805.9<u>9</u>7 → 806.00

  b) 45 578.9<u>20</u>27 → 45 578.92

  c) 12<u>4</u>3.304 → 1240

2. a) <u>1</u>273.097 → 1000

  b) <u>1</u>07.896 → 110

  c) 0.007 8<u>06</u>4 → 0.00781

3. a) $\frac{32.8 \times 15.9}{8.9} = \frac{30 \times 20}{10} = 60$

  b) $6 \times 2 = 12\,\text{m}^2$

4. £0.27 → £0.30

  $\frac{£9}{£0.30} = \frac{900}{30} = 30$

  Yes, she has enough.

5. a) 1.34×10^4

  b) 3.45×10^{-3}

Page 25

1. a) $3.25 \times 2.83 = 9.1975\,\text{m}^2 \approx 9.20\,\text{m}^2$
  Each measurement is given to 3 s.f., so round the answer to 3 s.f.

  b) £35.62 ÷ 15 = £2.3746 ≈ £2.37 per metre
  The question involves money, so round to the nearest pence.

2. Degree of accuracy = 1 kg, so add and subtract 0.5 kg
  Largest mass: 98 + 0.5 = 98.5 kg
  Smallest mass: 98 − 0.5 = 97.5 kg

3. Degree of accuracy = 0.01 litre, so add and subtract 0.005 litre
  Largest volume: 1.25 + 0.005 = 1.255 litres
  Smallest volume: 1.25 − 0.005 = 1.245 litres

4. Largest possible base: 10.5 cm
  Largest possible height: 30.5 cm

Largest possible area: 10.5 × 30.5 ÷ 2 = 160.125 cm²

Page 27

1.

	Type	Terms	Variables	Coefficients	Constants
$s^2 + 3su - 4$	Expression	s^2 $3su$ -4	s u	1 (for s^2) 3 (for su)	-4
$3k + 4 = 10$	Equation	$3k$ 4	k	3 (for $3k$)	4 10
$2x + 3x \equiv 5x$	Identity	$2x$ $3x$ $5x$	x	2 (for $2x$) 3 (for $3x$) 5 (for $5x$)	None

2. a) $3x + 5y - 5x + 3 = -2x + 5y + 3$

  b) $4j^2 + 3j - 1 + 2j - 4 = 4j^2 + 5j - 5$

  c) $5k - 7 + 3k - 9k + 1 = -k - 6$

3. $5x$ where x is the side length

4. $15s + 25t$, where s is the number of t-shirts and t is the number of trousers

Page 29

1. a) $x = 2y + 4z - 1$

  $x = (2 \times 4) + (4 \times 5) - 1$

  $x = 8 + 20 - 1 = 27$

  b) $R = \frac{3x - 2t}{2}$

  $R = \frac{(3 \times 2) - (2 \times 1)}{2}$

  $R = \frac{6-2}{2} = \frac{4}{2} = 2$

2. $S = \frac{D}{T} = \frac{240}{4} = 60\,\text{mph}$

3. $V = \frac{1}{3}(a^2 \times h)$

  $V = \frac{1}{3}(2^2 \times 3)$

  $V = \frac{1}{3} \times 12 = 4\,\text{cm}^3$

Page 31

1. a) $4(j - 5) = 4j - 20$

  b) $-2(k - 1) = -2k + 2$

  c) $3(2m + 4) = 6m + 12$

2. $3(x - 3) - 2(x + 4) = 3x - 9 - 2x - 8 = x - 17$

3. a) $(x - 3)(x + 5) = x^2 + 5x - 3x - 15$
  $= x^2 + 2x - 15$

  b) $(2x + 1)(3x - 5) = 6x^2 - 10x + 3x - 5$
  $= 6x^2 - 7x - 5$

  c) $(2m - 3)(3m + 1) = 6m^2 + 2m - 9m - 3$
  $= 6m^2 - 7m - 3$

Page 33

1. a) $2(x + 2)$

  b) $3(a + 3b)$

  c) $5x(1 + 4y)$

2. a) $(x + 3)(x + 1)$

  b) $(k - 2)(k + 3)$

  c) $(x - 4)(x + 1)$

3. a) $(x + 4)(x - 4)$

  b) $(x + 13)(x - 13)$

Page 35

1. a) $x \times x \times x \times x \times x \times x$

  b) $3 \times k \times k \times k \times k$

  c) $5 \times 5 \times 5 \times j \times j \times j$

2. a) $k^2 \times k^8 = k^{(2 + 8)} = k^{10}$

  b) $\frac{j^8}{j^3} = j^{8-3} = j^5$

  c) $\frac{x^3 \times x}{x^5} = \frac{x^{(3+1)}}{x^5} = \frac{x^4}{x^5} = x^{4-5} = x^{-1} = \frac{1}{x}$

3. a) $2p^5 \times 3p^{-3} = 6 \times p^{(5-3)} = 6p^2$

  b) $\frac{(2m)^3 \times m}{4m^2} = \frac{2^3 \times m^3 \times m}{4m^2} = \frac{8m^4}{4m^2}$
$$= 2m^{(4-2)} = 2m^2$$

  c) $(3k^4)^2 \div k^{10} = (3^2 \times (k^4)^2) \div k^{10} = 9k^8 \div k^{10}$
$$= 9k^{-2} = \frac{9}{k^2}$$

Page 37

1. a) $C = 130 + 65h$, where C is the total cost and h is the number of hours worked

  b) $C = 130 + (65 \times 4) = £390$

2. a) $T = 3a + 2b$, where T is the total, a is the number of boxes of pens and b is the number of boxes of pencils.

  b) $T = (3 \times 4) + (2 \times 5) = £22$

3. a) $A = \frac{1}{2}(a + b)h$
$$2A = h(a + b)$$
$$\frac{2A}{h} = a + b$$
$$\frac{2A}{h} - a = b$$

  b) $\frac{2A}{h} - a = b$
$$\frac{2 \times 78}{6} - 11 = b$$
$$b = 15\,\text{cm}$$

Page 39

1. a)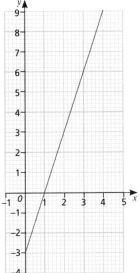

  b)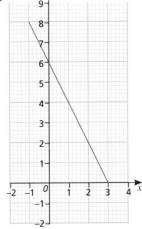

2. a) Two points are $(0, 1)$ and $(1, 4)$.

  Gradient $= \dfrac{\text{Difference in } y \text{ values}}{\text{Difference in } x \text{ values}}$
$$= \frac{4 - 1}{1 - 0} = \frac{3}{1} = 3$$

  b) Two points are $(1, 8)$ and $(3, 1)$.

  Gradient $= \dfrac{\text{Difference in } y \text{ values}}{\text{Difference in } x \text{ values}}$
$$= \frac{1 - 8}{3 - 1} = \frac{-7}{2} = -3.5$$

Page 41

1. a) $(0, -3)$

  b) $(-1, 0)$ and $(3, 0)$

  c) $(1, -4)$

2.

x	−4	−3	−2	−1	0
y	6	0	−2	0	6

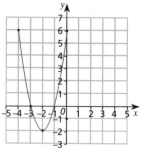

Page 43

1. When $x = -2$: $y = (-2)^3 + 1 = -8 + 1 = -7$

  When $x = -1$: $y = (-1)^3 + 1 = -1 + 1 = 0$

  When $x = 0$: $y = 0^3 + 1 = 1$

  When $x = 1$: $y = 1^3 + 1 = 2$

  When $x = 2$: $y = 2^3 + 1 = 9$

x	−2	−1	0	1	2
y	−7	0	1	2	9

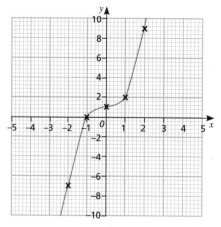

2. When $x = -3$: $y = \frac{3}{-3} = -1$

  When $x = -2$: $y = \frac{3}{-2} = -\frac{3}{2} = -1\frac{1}{2}$

  When $x = -1$: $y = \frac{3}{-1} = -3$

When $x = 1$: $y = \frac{3}{1} = 3$

When $x = 2$: $y = \frac{3}{2} = 1\frac{1}{2}$

When $x = 3$: $y = \frac{3}{3} = 1$

x	−3	−2	−1	1	2	3
y	−1	−1.5	−3	3	1.5	1

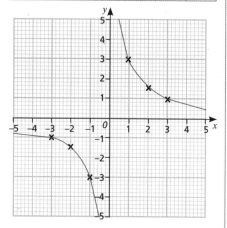

Page 45

1. a) 10 minutes on his way to the shops + 25 minutes at the shops = 35 minutes

  b) The distance is the difference in the y coordinates $(12 - 0 = 12)$ and the time is the difference in the x coordinates $(90 - 70 = 20)$

  20 minutes = $\frac{1}{3}$ of an hour

  Speed = $\frac{\text{distance}}{\text{time}}$ = $12 \div \frac{1}{3}$ = $12 \times 3 = 36\,\text{mph}$

2. a) Graph 3 (the container has straight vertical sides so each part of the graph is straight; it fills up slowly at first then quickly)

  b) Graph 4 (the container has straight vertical sides so the graph is straight; it fills up slower than container D)

  c) Graph 2 (the container has slanted sides so the rate it fills up is constantly changing; it fills up more quickly at first, then slows down)

  d) Graph 1 (the container has straight vertical sides so the graph is straight; it fills up faster than container B)

3. a) Between 1819 and 1820

  b) 1815

Page 47

1. a) $x = 4$ **b)** $x = 3$ **c)** $x = 4$ **d)** $x = -4$

2. a) $x = -3$ **b)** $x = 5$ **c)** $x = 5$ **d)** $x = 7$

Page 49

1. a) $x^2 - 5x - 24 = 0$
$(x + 3)(x - 8) = 0$
$x = -3$ or $x = 8$

b) $x^2 = 15 - 2x$
$x^2 + 2x - 15 = 0$
$(x - 3)(x + 5) = 0$
$x = 3$ or $x = -5$

c) $x^2 - 10x = -16$
$x^2 - 10x + 16 = 0$
$(x - 2)(x - 8) = 0$
$x = 2$ or $x = 8$

2. a) $x - 4 = 0$ or $x + 5 = 0$
$(x - 4)(x + 5) = 0$
$x^2 + 5x - 4x - 20 = 0$
$x^2 + x - 20 = 0$

b) $x - 3 = 0$
$(x - 3)(x - 3) = 0$
$x^2 - 6x + 9 = 0$

Page 51

1. a) *Using substitution:*
(1) $4x - y = 1$
(2) $y + 3 = 2x$

$y = 2x - 3$ Rearrange (2)
$4x - (2x - 3) = -1$ Substitute into (1)
$2x + 3 = 1$ Solve for x
$2x = -2$
$x = -1$

$y = 2x - 3$ Substitute x into (2)
$y = (2 \times -1) - 3$ Solve for y
$y = -5$
Solution is $x = -1$ and $y = -5$

b) *Using elimination:*
(1) $2x + 3y = 9$
(2) $4x - 9y = 3$
(3) = (1) × 2 = $4x + 6y = 18$

$4x + 6y = 18$
$\underline{-(4x - 9y = 3)}$ Subtract (3) from (1)
$15y = 15$ Solve for y
$y = 1$

$2x + (3 \times 1) = 9$ Substitute y into (1)
$2x + 3 = 9$ Solve for x
$2x = 6$
$x = 3$
Solution is $x = 3$ and $y = 1$

2. x value between $x = 1.2$ and $x = 1.6$
y value between $y = -0.7$ and $y = -1.1$

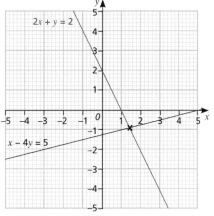

Page 53

1. a) $2x + 1 + 8x + 5 + 2x - 6 = 180$
$12x = 180$

b) $12x = 180$
$x = 15$

c) $2x + 1 = (2 \times 15) + 1 = 31°$
$8x + 5 = (8 \times 15) + 5 = 125°$
$2x - 6 = (2 \times 15) - 6 = 24°$

2. a) $A = (x + 1)(x - 2)$
$A = x^2 - x - 2$

b) $x^2 - x - 2 = 70$
$x^2 - x - 72 = 0$
$(x - 9)(x + 8) = 0$
$x = 9$ or $x = -8$. x cannot be negative, so $x = 9$

c) When $x = 9$, $x - 2 = 9 - 2 = 7$
When $x = 9$, $x + 1 = 9 + 1 = 10$
Sides are 7 cm and 10 cm

Page 55

1. a)

b)

c)

2. a) $3x + 2 < 8$
$3x < 6$
$x < 2$

b) $-7 > 8 - 3x$
$-7 + 3x > 8$
$3x > 15$
$x > 5$

c) $2x + 1 \leqslant 3x + 2$
$1 \leqslant x + 2$
$-1 \leqslant x$
$x \geqslant -1$

d) $15 < 5x \leqslant 20$
Split into two: $15 < 5x$ and $5x \leqslant 20$
$3 < x$ and $x \leqslant 4$
Combine into a double inequality: $3 < x \leqslant 4$

Page 57

1. a) 2, 7, 12, 17, **22**, **27**
Term-to-term rule: Start at 2 and add 5

b) 12, 8, 4, 0, **−4**, **−8**
Term-to-term rule: Start at 12 and subtract 4

c) 9, 16, 23, 30, **37**, **44**
Term-to-term rule: Start at 9 and add 7

d) 56, 48, 40, **32**, **24**
Term-to-term rule: Start at 56 and subtract 8

2. When $n = 1$: $(4 \times 1) + 5 = 9$
When $n = 2$: $(4 \times 2) + 5 = 13$
When $n = 3$: $(4 \times 3) + 5 = 17$
When $n = 10$: $(4 \times 10) + 5 = 45$

3. a) $2n + 3$

b) $-3n + 20$

Page 59

1. a) Missing terms: 1, $\frac{1}{3}$
Common ratio: $\frac{1}{3}$

b) Missing terms: 48, 96
Common ratio: 2

c) Missing terms: 54, 18
Common ratio: 3

2. a) 28, 39
b) −8, −10

3. When $n = 1$: $2 \times (1^3) + 5 = 2 + 5 = 7$
When $n = 2$: $2 \times (2^3) + 5 = 16 + 5 = 21$
When $n = 3$: $2 \times (3^3) + 5 = 54 + 5 = 59$

4. a) 10, 18, 28
b) −6, −10, −16

Page 61

1. a) $13 \times 100 = 1300\,cm$

b) $130 \div 10 = 13\,mm$

2. $1.37 \times 10 = 13.7\,mm$

3. a) $13 \times 100^2 = 130\,000\,cm^2$

b) $130 \div 10^2 = 1.3\,cm^2$

4. $56\,400\,000 \div 1000^2 = 56.4\,km^2$

5. $35\,000 \div 100^3 = 0.035 = 3.5 \times 10^{-2}\,m^3$

Page 63

1. $5 \div 2 = 2.5$

2. a) Sides are 10 units and 6 units with the fireplace being 1 unit by 2 units.

The actual distances are 5 m, 3 m and 0.5×1 m for the fireplace.

The area is then $5\,m \times 3\,m - (0.5\,m \times 1\,m)$
$= 14.5\,m^2$

b) 15 m² is needed
$15 \times 14 = £210$

Page 65

1. a) $1 : 4$

b) $2 : 5$

c) $2\,cm : 100\,000\,cm \Rightarrow 1 : 50\,000$

d) $15\,000\,g : 800\,g \Rightarrow 75 : 4$

2. a) Bottle A:
squash : water $= 500\,ml : 1500\,ml \Rightarrow \frac{1}{3} : 1$

Bottle B:
squash : water $= 160 : 640 \Rightarrow \frac{1}{4} : 1$

b) Bottle A has a higher amount of squash per ml of water because $\frac{1}{3} > \frac{1}{4}$

3. a) $15 : 0.5 \Rightarrow 150 : 5 \Rightarrow 30 : 1$

b) $\frac{2}{5} = \frac{14}{35}$ and $\frac{4}{7} = \frac{20}{35}$
$\frac{14}{35} : \frac{20}{35}$
$= 14 : 20$
$= 7 : 10$

Page 67

1. Charity X = £480
Charity Y = £720

2. a) Charity A = £18
Charity C = £36

b) £108

3. a) $\frac{4}{5}$

b) $120 \times \frac{4}{5} = 96$ adults

Page 69

1. a) 150 g **b)** 300 ml

c) 3 eggs **d)** 75 ml

2. £1.40 ÷ 70 g = £0.02 per gram
£10.00 ÷ 1000 g = £0.01 per gram
The 1 kg tub is the better deal.

3. £6.00 ÷ 200 ml = £0.03 per ml
£10.00 ÷ 500 ml = £0.02 per ml
The 500 ml bottle is the better deal.

Page 71

1.

Percentage	Fraction	Decimal
20%	$\frac{20}{100} = \frac{1}{5}$	0.2
45%	$\frac{45}{100} = \frac{9}{20}$	0.45
62%	$\frac{62}{100} = \frac{31}{50}$	0.62
55%	$\frac{11}{20}$	0.55
12%	$\frac{12}{100} = \frac{3}{25}$	0.12
37.5%	$\frac{3}{8}$	0.375

2. 10% of 600 g = 60 g
30% of 600 g = 3 × 60 g = 180 g

3. 10% of £80 = £8
5% of £80 = £4
15% of £80 = £8 + £4 = £12

4. 26.5 km = 26 500 m
$\frac{265}{26500} = \frac{1}{100} = 1\%$

Page 73

1. £15 − £12 = £3
$\frac{3}{15} = \frac{1}{5} = 20\%$

2. £1200 × 1.03 = £1236

3. 20% increase so multiplier is 1.2
£3000 ÷ 1.2 = £2500

4. 15% discount means paying 85% of the full price, so the multiplier is 0.85
£21.25 ÷ 0.85 = £25

Page 75

1. Time = Distance ÷ Speed = 140 ÷ 40 = 3.5 h

2. 11:05 to 13:15 is 2 hours and 10 minutes
$= 2\frac{1}{6}$ hours
Distance = Speed × Time = $2\frac{1}{6}$ × 924 = 2002 km

3. 11 kg = 11 000 g
Volume = Mass ÷ Density
11 000 g ÷ 19 g/cm³ = 579 cm³

4. Pressure = Force ÷ Area
60 N ÷ 0.012 m² = 5000 N/m²

5. Mass = Rate × Time
0.6 g/s × 180 s = 108 g

Page 77

1. $y = 3x$
$y = 3 × 4 = 12$

2. The ratio between the values is 4.
The error is where $x = 4$. It should be $y = 16$.

3. $y = \frac{18}{x}$
$y = \frac{18}{4} = \frac{9}{2}$ or $4\frac{1}{2}$

4. Ink used is inversely proportional to the number of pages printed.

At 600 pages a day, ink lasts for 3 weeks.

The number of pages printed has been divided by 3 (600 ÷ 3 = 200), so to find the number of weeks, multiply by 3.

At 200 pages a day, ink lasts for 3 × 3 = 9 weeks

Page 79

1. a) $S = 2000m$ where S is the number of steps taken and m is the number of miles walked.

b) $V = 500 − 50y$ where V is the value of the phone and y is the number of years.

c) $V = 12m$, where V is the volume of water and m is the number of minutes.

2. a) 7 miles

b) He drives faster from the coffee shop to work because the line is steeper than for the journey from home to the coffee shop.

c) Gradient = $\frac{\text{change in } y}{\text{change in } x}$

$= \frac{20 − 7}{50 − 30} = \frac{13}{20}$ miles per minute

$\frac{13}{20} × 60 = 39$ mph

Page 81

1. $A = 1500 × (1 + \frac{3}{100})^5 = £1738.91$

2. $A = 25 × 1.12^3 = 35$ foxes

3. $A = 1200 × 0.84^4 = £597.45$

4. $A = 20\,000 × 0.85^{12} = £2844.84$

Page 83

1.

2.

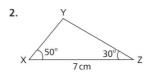

Page 85

1.

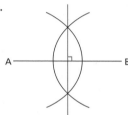

2.

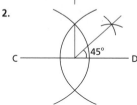

Page 87

1. a) $x = 120°$. They are allied angles.

b) $y = 50°$. They are corresponding angles.

c) $z = 70°$. It is vertically opposite the allied angle to 110°, or it is on a straight line with an angle corresponding to 110°.

2. Interior angles of the pentagon:
$360° ÷ 5 = 72°$
$180° − 72° = 108°$

Interior angles of the octagon:
$360° ÷ 8 = 45°$
$180° − 45° = 135°$

x and the interior angles of the pentagon and octagon sum to 360° as they are angles around a point.
$360° − (108° + 135°) = 117°$

Page 89

1. a) $180° − 38° = 142°$
(angles in a triangle sum to 180°)

$142° ÷ 2 = 71°$
(base angles of an isosceles triangle are equal)

$a = 71°$ and $b = 71°$

b) $d = 180° − 118° = 62°$
(angles on a straight line sum to 180°)

Angle $c = 180° − (90° + 62°) = 28°$
(angles in a triangle sum to 180°)

c) $e = 180° − 103° = 77°$
(angles on a straight line sum to 180°)

$f = 180° − (52° + 77°) = 51°$
(angles in a triangle sum to 180°)

2. *Any one from:* kite; isosceles trapezium

3. a) $b = 75°$ (one pair of equal angles in a kite)
$360° − (2 × 75°) = 210°$
(angles in a quadrilateral sum to 360°)
$a + 2a = 210°$
$3a = 210°$, so $a = 70°$

b) $e = 57°$ (base angles of an isosceles trapezium are equal)
$c = 180° − 57° = 123°$ (allied angle with 57°)
$d = 123°$ (allied with angle e)

Page 91

1. a) E and J

b) H

c) G

2. a) Yes, by ASA

b) No, the side lengths that are equal are not corresponding sides

c) Yes, by SAS

d) Yes, by SSS

Page 93

1. a) Translation 5 units to the left and 1 unit up, or $\binom{-5}{1}$.

b) Move each vertex 1 to the right and down 3.

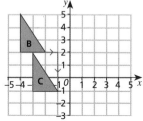

2.

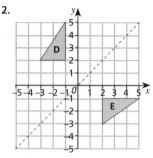

3. Reflection in the line $y = 4$

4.

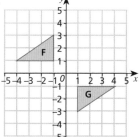

5. Rotation 90° anticlockwise about (–1, –1)

Page 95

1. *Enlargements can be placed anywhere on the grid.*

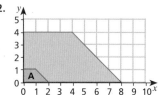

2.

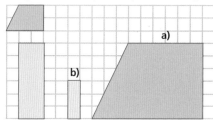

3. Enlargement by a scale factor of $\frac{1}{2}$ from point (9, 6)

Page 97

1. a) Cuboid

b) Hexagonal prism

c) Triangular-based pyramid / Tetrahedron

d) Cone

2.

	Shape	Faces	Edges	Vertices
a)	Cuboid	6	12	8
b)	Hexagonal prism	8	18	12
c)	Triangular-based pyramid	4	6	4
d)	Cone	2	1	1

3. a) Rectangle

b) Pentagon

c) Octagon

Page 99

1. a)   **b)**   **c)**

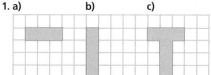

2. a)

b)

Page 101

1.

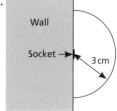

2. a) 300°

b) 130°

c) 020°

Page 103

1. a) Perimeter =
4 + 1 + 1 + 1 + 1 + 1 + 1 + 1 + 1 + 2
= 14 cm

b) Perimeter =
4.3 + 3.1 + 1.2 + 1.7 + 1.9 + 1.7 + 1.2 + 3.1
= 18.2 m

2. a) Area = $\frac{1}{2} \times 4.2 \times 8.6 = 18.06$ mm^2

b) Area = $\frac{1}{2} \times (4.6 + 5.8) \times 1.9 = 9.88$ cm^2

c) Area = $1.6 \times 3.2 = 5.12$ cm^2

d) Area of triangle = $\frac{1}{2} \times 14.9 \times 6 = 44.7$ m^2
Area of rectangle = $30.2 \times 12 = 362.4$ m^2
Total = 407.1 m^2

Page 105

1. a) Diameter   **b)** Tangent

  c) Radius   **d)** Arc

  e) Sector   **f)** Chord

2. a) Circumference = $(3.2 \times 2) \times \pi = 20.1$ cm
(to 1 d.p.)
Area = $\pi \times (3.2)^2 = 32.2$ cm^2 (to 1 d.p.)

  b) Circumference = $5.8 \times \pi = 18.2$ m (to 1 d.p.)
Radius = $5.8 \div 2 = 2.9$ m
Area = $\pi \times (2.9)^2 = 26.4$ m^2 (to 1 d.p.)

3. a) Arc length = $\frac{\text{angle at centre}}{360°} \times$ circumference
of circle

$= \frac{120}{360} \times 2 \times \pi \times 5 = 10.47$ cm (to 2 d.p.)

  b) Area of sector = $\frac{\text{angle at centre}}{360°} \times$ area of circle

$= \frac{120}{360} \times \pi \times 5^2 = 26.18$ cm^2 (to 2 d.p.)

Page 107

1. a) $2 \times (5 \times 4) = 40$ cm^2 and $2 \times (5 \times 2) = 20$ cm^2
and $2 \times (4 \times 2) = 16$ cm^2

$40 + 20 + 16 = 76$ cm^2

  b) Area of pentagon = 27.5 cm^2
Area of rectangle = $4 \times 10 = 40$ cm^2
Total surface area = $(2 \times 27.5) + (5 \times 40)$
$= 255$ cm^2

2. a) Volume = $l \times w \times h = 5 \times 4 \times 2 = 40$ cm^3

  b) Volume = area of cross-section $\times$ depth
$= 27.5$ cm$^2 \times 10$ cm $= 275$ cm^3

3. Volume = $\frac{4}{3}\pi r^3$

$= \frac{4}{3} \times \pi \times 6^3$

$= 288\pi$ m^3 or 904.8 m^3

4. Volume of pyramid = $\frac{1}{3} \times$ area of base $\times$
vertical height $= \frac{1}{3} \times (5 \times 4) \times 9 = 60$ cm^3

Page 109

1. The corresponding angles are the same.
$6 \div 3 = 2$ and $10 \div 5 = 2$ and $8 \div 4 = 2$

The ratio of each corresponding side is 2, so
the triangles are similar.

2. Triangle ABC is similar to triangle ADE with
side AC corresponding to side AE.

Side BC corresponds to side DE, so the scale
factor is $16 \div 10 = 1.6$

So side AE = $8 \times 1.6 = 12.8$ cm

Side CE = $12.8 - 8 = 4.8$ cm

3. a) 3.75 cm = 375 km (370–380 km is acceptable)

  b) 2.25 cm = 225 km (220–230 km is acceptable)

Page 111

1. a) $10^2 + 12^2 = c^2$
$c = \sqrt{10^2 + 12^2} = 15.62$ cm (to 2 d.p.)

  b) $a^2 + 24^2 = 25^2$
$a = \sqrt{25^2 - 24^2} = 7$ cm

2. Height of the triangle:
$a^2 + 8^2 = 17^2$
$a = \sqrt{17^2 - 8^2} = 15$
Area of the triangle: $A = \frac{1}{2}bh$
$A = \frac{1}{2} \times 16 \times 15 = 120$ cm^2

3. Find the base of the rectangle by using the
diagonal and Pythagoras' theorem:
$a^2 + 12^2 = 37^2$
$a = \sqrt{37^2 - 12^2} = 35$ cm
Area of the rectangle = $12 \times 35 = 420$ cm^2

Page 113

1. a) $\sin(42°) = \frac{x}{10}$
$x = 10 \times \sin(42°) = 6.69$ cm (to 2 d.p.)

  b) $\tan(35°) = \frac{8}{x}$
$8 = \tan(35°) \times x$
$x = \frac{8}{\tan(35°)} = 11.43$ cm (to 2 d.p.)

  c) $\cos(x) = \frac{4}{8}$
$\cos^{-1}\left(\frac{1}{2}\right) = 60°$

2. Draw a right-angled triangle with
the given information:

$\tan(60°) = \frac{x}{20}$
$x = 20 \times \tan(60°) = 34.641015...$
Building's height is 35 m.

Page 115

1. $\begin{pmatrix} 5 \\ -3 \end{pmatrix}$ means to translate the point by 5 units in
the x direction and -3 units in the y direction.
$1 + 5 = 6$ and $2 - 3 = -1$
Coordinates of B are (6, −1).

2. a) $\overrightarrow{BC} = -\mathbf{a}$

  b) $\overrightarrow{BD} = \overrightarrow{BC} + \overrightarrow{CD} = -\mathbf{a} - \mathbf{b}$

  c) $\overrightarrow{CO} = -\mathbf{b} + \mathbf{a}$

3. a) $\overrightarrow{BA} = \overrightarrow{BO} + \overrightarrow{OA}$
$= -\mathbf{b} + \mathbf{a}$
$= \mathbf{a} - \mathbf{b}$

  b) $\overrightarrow{AC} = \overrightarrow{AO} + \overrightarrow{OC}$
$= -\overrightarrow{OA} + \overrightarrow{OC}$
$= -\mathbf{a} + 2\mathbf{a} - 3\mathbf{b}$
$= \mathbf{a} - 3\mathbf{b}$

Page 117

1. a) Impossible **b)** Even chance

  c) Certain **d)** Unlikely

2. $\frac{2}{5}$

3. $P(M) = \frac{\text{total number of Ms}}{\text{total number of letters}} = \frac{2}{11}$

4. 19% (or $\frac{19}{100}$ or 0.19)

5. P(yellow) = $\frac{2}{5}$

  P(not yellow) = $1 - \frac{2}{5} = \frac{3}{5}$ (or 0.6 or 60%)

Page 119

1. a)

Colour	Blue	Red	Green	Yellow
Frequency	15	20	18	7
Relative frequency	0.25	0.33	0.30	0.12

b) Yes, the theoretical probability of yellow is 0.25, so the relative frequency of yellow is quite a bit lower than you would expect. 60 is a reasonable number of trials, so yes, the spinner is likely to be biased. She should do more trials to confirm.

2. a) Relative frequency =

$\frac{\text{Number of favourable outcomes (red admirals)}}{\text{Total number of trials (total butterflies)}}$

$= \frac{26}{100} = 0.26$

b) 0.26 × 700 = 182 red admirals

Page 121

1.

		Dice 1				
		1	**2**	**3**	**4**	**5**	**6**
	1	1	2	3	4	5	6
	2	2	4	6	8	10	12
Dice 2	**3**	3	6	9	12	15	18
	4	4	8	12	16	20	24
	5	5	10	15	20	25	30
	6	6	12	18	24	30	36

2. *Any suitable answer, e.g.*

		Spinner 1			
		1	**2**	**3**	**4**
	Red	R, 1	R, 2	R, 3	R, 4
Spinner 2	Red	R, 1	R, 2	R, 3	R, 4
	Yellow	Y, 1	Y, 2	Y, 3	Y, 4
	Blue	B, 1	B, 2	B, 3	B, 4

3. $P(R, 4) = \frac{2}{16} = \frac{1}{8}$

4. $P(R, 4) = P(R) \times P(4) = \frac{1}{2} \times \frac{1}{4} = \frac{1}{8}$

Page 123

1. a)

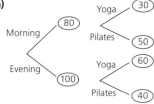

b) P(Pilates) = $\frac{90}{180} = \frac{1}{2}$

2. a)

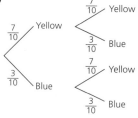

b) P(YY) = $\frac{7}{10} \times \frac{7}{10} = \frac{49}{100}$

Page 125

1. a) 40 + 12 + 28 + 10 = 90

b) 40

c) 28 + 12 = 40 play rugby out of 90 total

  So P(rugby) = $\frac{40}{90}$ or $\frac{4}{9}$

2. a) Calculations:

  100 − 12 = 88 take a tram and/or a bus

  35 + 68 = 103

  103 − 88 = 15 take a bus and a tram

  35 − 15 = 20 take only the tram

  68 − 15 = 53 take only the bus

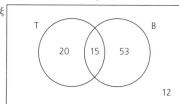

b) P(tram and bus) = $\frac{15}{100}$ (or 0.15 or 15%)

Page 127

1. a) i) Numerical (discrete)

    ii) Numerical (continuous)

    iii) Categorical

    iv) Numerical (continuous)

  b) They should ask people from a variety of age groups and choose visitors randomly.

2. Hypothesis:

We think the queue times are longest between 1 pm and 2 pm.

Plan and collect the data:

Track the length of time visitors are in the queue during each hour of the day.

Give visitors a card with the time they entered the queue to record the queuing time.

Process and represent the data:

Draw an appropriate chart, e.g. time series or bar graph.

Work out the mean and range of queuing time between each hour of the day.

Interpret and discuss the results:

Look at the chart and compare the means and ranges to draw conclusions.

Revise the hypothesis and repeat the cycle.

Page 129

1.

Sandwich	Tally	Frequency
Tuna	||||	4
Cheese	|||| |	6
Ham	|||	3
Beef	||||	5
		Total = 18

2.

	Physiotherapy	Medication	Total
Recovered	57	10	67
Not recovered	8	5	13
Total	65	15	80

3. a) 112 students

  b) Dance

  c) Gymnastics and Drama

Page 131

1.

Type of book	Number of students	Angle (°)
Non-fiction	108	$\frac{108}{1080} \times 360° = \textbf{36°}$
Fantasy	162	$\frac{162}{1080} \times 360° = \textbf{54°}$
Mystery	270	$\frac{270}{1080} \times 360° = \textbf{90°}$
Historical fiction	324	$\frac{324}{1080} \times 360° = \textbf{108°}$
General fiction	216	$\frac{216}{1080} \times 360° = \textbf{72°}$
Total	**1080**	**360°**

2.

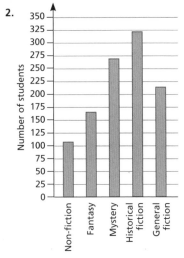

Page 133

1.

x	f	Cumulative frequency	$f \times x$
3	1	1	$1 \times 3 = 3$
4	9	$1 + 9 = 10$	$9 \times 4 = 36$
5	6	$10 + 6 = 16$	$6 \times 5 = 30$
6	3	$16 + 3 = 19$	$3 \times 6 = 18$
Total	**19**		**87**

a) 4

b) Mean = $\frac{\text{sum of } f \times x}{\text{sum of } f} = \frac{87}{19}$

    = 4.58 (to 2 d.p.)

c) 4

d) Range = $6 - 3 = 3$

2. a) $2 < x \leq 4$

b) There are 51 values so the median is the

$\frac{51 + 1}{2} = 26$th value

26th value is in the class is $2 < x \leq 4$

c)

Class	Frequency, f	Mid-class value, x	Frequency × Mid-class value (fx)
$0 < x \leq 2$	10	$\frac{0 + 2}{2} = 1$	$10 \times 1 = 10$
$2 < x \leq 4$	21	$\frac{2 + 4}{2} = 3$	$3 \times 21 = 63$
$4 < x \leq 6$	13	$\frac{4 + 6}{2} = 5$	$5 \times 13 = 65$
$6 < x \leq 8$	7	$\frac{6 + 8}{2} = 7$	$7 \times 7 = 49$
Total	51		187

$\text{Mean} = \frac{\text{sum of } f \times x}{\text{sum of } f} = \frac{187}{51} = 3.67$

Page 135

1. a)

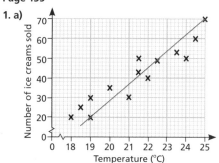

b) Draw a line from $x = 23°C$ to the line of best fit and follow it to the y-axis.

53 ice creams (answers from 51 to 55 would be acceptable)

2.

Pages 136–141

1. a)

b) The pattern starts at 5 and goes up in 2s, the nth term rule is $2n + 3$.

Then the 10th term is $(2 \times 10) + 3 = 23$

Or count up to the 10th pattern:
5, 7, 9, 11, 13, …

c) The pattern always has an odd number of sticks and 84 is even.

2. a) $7x$ **b)** 4

c) $x = 6$ **d)** $x = -6$

3. a) 9

b) 13

c) 9, 15

d) 9, 18, 27

4. a) When $x = 0$, $y = (3 \times 0) - 4 = -4$

When $x = 2$, $y = (3 \times 2) - 4 = 2$

x	-1	0	1	2	3
y	-7	-4	-1	2	5

b)

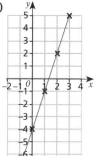

5.

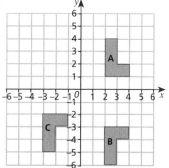

6. a) $x^2 + 7x + 12 = (x + 3)(x + 4)$

b) $x^2 + 7x + 12 = 0$
$(x + 3)(x + 4) = 0$
$x + 3 = 0$ or $x + 4 = 0$
$x = -3$ or $x = -4$

7. Fridge World: £810 ÷ 3 = £270
£810 − £270 = £540
Fridge Bargains: 12 × £40 = £480, plus £100
deposit = £580
The Electric Store: £500 × 0.2 = £100
£500 + £100 = £600
Fridge World is the cheapest.

8. $P = A\left(1 + \frac{r}{100}\right)^n = 2500 \times \left(1 + \frac{3}{100}\right)^3$

$= 2500 \times (1.03)^3 = £2731.82$
Or
Year 1: £2500 × 1.03 = £2575
Year 2: £2575 × 1.03 = £2652.25
Year 3: £2652.25 × 1.03 = £2731.82

9. $A = \frac{1}{2}(4 + 9) \times 5 = 32.5\,\text{cm}^2$

10.a) Angle x combined with the angle of 34°
makes an alternate angle with the angle
given as 47°, then $x + 34° = 47°$

$x = 47° - 34° = 13°$

b) Angle y is allied (or co-interior) to 34°.
So $y = 180° - 34° = 146°$

11. a) Area of a circle: $A = \pi r^2$, so the area of a
semicircle is $A = \frac{1}{2} \times \pi r^2$

$A = \frac{1}{2} \times \pi \times 4.2^2 = 27.71\,\text{cm}^2$ (2 d.p.)

b) Perimeter is half the circumference of a
circle plus the distance of the diameter,
$d = 2 \times 4.2 = 8.4$

$C = \pi \times d$ so the circumference of the
circular part $C = \frac{1}{2} \times \pi \times d = \frac{1}{2} \times \pi \times 8.4$
$= 13.194\,68...$
Perimeter of the semicircle is therefore
$13.196\,48... + 8.4 = 21.59\,\text{cm}$ (2 d.p.)

12. a)

Favourite sport	Tally	Frequency
Football	JHT II	7
Cricket	JHT	5
Rugby	JHT I	6
Swimming	II	2

b) Football

c)

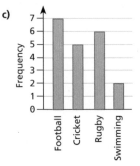

13. x corresponds to the longer side of the
trapezium. Use the shorter sides to find the
scale factor 12 ÷ 8 = 1.5
10 × 1.5 = 15 cm, so $x = 15$ cm

14. a)

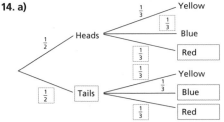

b) P(tails and yellow) = P(tails) × P(yellow)
$= \frac{1}{2} \times \frac{1}{3} = \frac{1}{6}$

15. a) Circle around the student at (57, 2). It doesn't
follow the trend of the rest of the points.

b) Line of best fit starting at or before (23, 1)
to (35, 1) and ending at or after (58, 5) to
(62, 5).

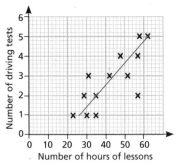

c) The greater the number of tests taken, the
greater the number of hours of lessons.

16. a) $x^2 + 9^2 = 15^2$

$x = \sqrt{15^2 - 9^2} = 12\,cm$

b) Use any of the trigonometric functions since you know all the sides.

$\cos(a) = \frac{9}{15}$

$\cos^{-1}\left(\frac{9}{15}\right) = 53.1301...°$

So $a = 53°$ (to the nearest degree)

17. £1300 ÷ 5 = £260

Pandas = £260 × 3 = £780

Elephants = £260 × 2 = £520

18. a) The net has two equal triangles and three rectangles.

Area of one triangle = $\frac{1}{2} \times 3 \times 4 = 6\,cm^2$

There are three rectangles:

$A_1 = 5 \times 10 = 50\,cm^2$

$A_2 = 4 \times 10 = 40\,cm^2$

$A_3 = 3 \times 10 = 30\,cm^2$

Total surface area = 6 + 6 + 50 + 40 + 30
= 132 cm²

b) Volume = Area of triangle × 10 = 6 × 10
= 60 cm³

19. They are congruent by Side, Angle, Side (SAS).

Notes

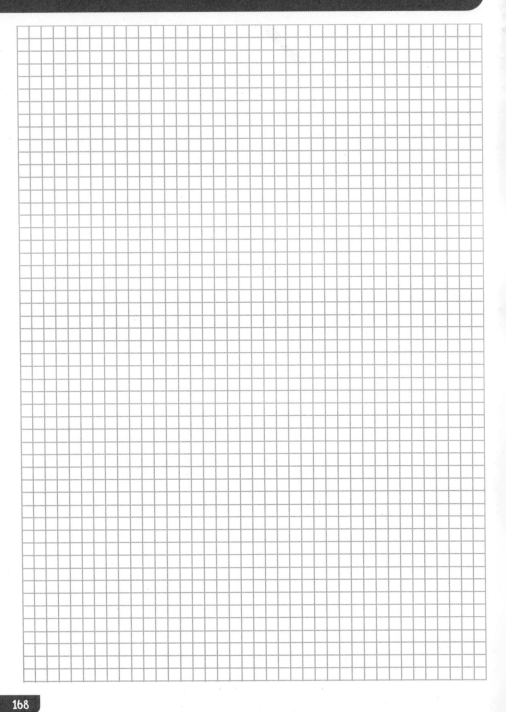